SHARI
A BEGINNERS' GUIDE
TO MAKING MONEY

'It is planning not gambling that produces profit and
security.'
Marcus Aurelius

'When I was a big star making lots of money, I needed
someone with experience to look after me. Now that
person's got the money and all I've got is the experience.'
Doris Day

'I'd like to live like a poor man with lots of money.'
Picasso

'I finally know what distinguishes man from the other
beasts: financial worries.'
Jules Renard

'Never invest your money in anything that eats or needs
repairing.'
Billy Rose

SHARES
A BEGINNERS' GUIDE
TO MAKING MONEY

'The guide explains how to speculate without losing
your shirt'
The Guardian

'Fun and profit for beginners'
Investment Adviser

'If you haven't already got in on the act – and want to – I
recommend Harold Baldwin's new book'
Woman's World

'Buying shares for the first time sounds complicated, but
need not be. Shares – A Beginners' Guide to Making
Money could help'
Sunday Express

SHARES
A BEGINNERS' GUIDE
TO MAKING MONEY

Thousands of men and women are making money from
shares. Many started with just a few hundred pounds.
Few had any previous experience on the stockmarket.

What is their recipe for success? You will find the answer
by reading Harold Baldwin's practical and interesting
advice. Then you can start making money for yourself.

WISEBUY PUBLICATIONS

SHARES
A BEGINNERS'
GUIDE
TO MAKING
MONEY

Harold Baldwin

WISEBUY PUBLICATIONS

First published 1986
Second extended edition 1987

**Further copies of SHARES – A BEGINNERS'
GUIDE TO MAKING MONEY can be
obtained from most bookshops. In case of
difficulty they can also be obtained from Dept
SH2, Wisebuy Publications, 25 West Cottages,
London NW6 1RJ price £2.95 plus 50p p&p
(UK) or Irish £4.25 (including p&p) or £6
(airmail).**

The information in this book has been checked for
accuracy and it is believed that it was correct at the
date of publication. However the author and
publishers cannot accept legal liability for any
errors or omissions, nor can they accept
responsibility with regard to the standing of any
organisation, or the quality of any product or
service, mentioned in the text. It is most important
that readers make their own checks on the
standing of investment advisers they employ.

British Library Cataloguing in Publication Data
Baldwin, Harold
    Shares: a beginners' guide to making money.
    —— 2nd ed.
    1. Investments —— Great Britain   2. Stocks
    —— Great Britain
    I. Title
    332.6'322   HG5432

ISBN 0-9509751-7-6

*Typesetting by MC Typeset, Chatham, Kent.
Printed in Great Britain by
The Guernsey Press Co Ltd, Guernsey, CI.*

Contents

Author's note

Many of the ideas in this book have been given to me by people presently involved in making money on the stock exchange. Yet more are well-known but anonymous market maxims. To all these successful money makers and everyone else who has assisted me in the production of this book I offer my grateful thanks.

If while reading the Guide, you come across some words you don't understand, turn to Chapter 17 for an explanation.

1

How To Get Started

You can make a lot of money on the stock market, but it means some work, a basic plan and above all gaining experience. And it can be fun too.

Most people have investments in the stock market through life policies, saving schemes, unit trusts, investment bonds and perhaps a few hundred TSB or British Telecom shares. Many such investors do not have the time or the inclination to actively participate in the stock market, but nevertheless wish to benefit from economic growth and protect themselves from the ravages of inflation. This Guide is not for them. *Unless, of course, they wish to make a lot of money as quickly as possible.*

This Guide is about speculating on the stock market. Does the word speculating frighten you? It should not, because there is an element of speculation in all investment. People talk about speculative shares, but there are times when it is hard to justify even buying Government stock or a *blue chip*, a share in a large established company, on any grounds except speculation.

The speculator aims to outperform the investor by studying the market, developing a skill and hopefully finding the occasional big winner. It is not that easy. If you think that it is, or simply a matter of luck, then you could lose a lot of money. However when the winning shares are listed in the newspapers it makes you feel how easy it might have been.

Some people are tempted by stories of shares bought for a few pence and sold for several pounds. They have little knowledge of how the market works, how to start trading in shares, or how to proceed once they hold them. When they get bitten and lose some of their hard-earned money they moan about bad luck and put their depleted capital back into the building society. Or, worse still, they become desperate and gamble wildly in an attempt to retrieve their losses.

Obviously, the speculator takes greater risks than the investor. You can be both an investor and a speculator. You would certainly be foolish to speculate all your money. But keep the two types of deals separate.

Before you make a purchase decide whether you are making an investment or a speculation – and keep your objective firmly in mind

How much money should you speculate?
First put aside and keep sufficient for your basic needs and insurance. After that it is a personal decision. Never borrow to play the market.

Move slowly. In fact, it is a good idea to play the market for a while without using any money. Buy and sell some shares in an imaginary way while keeping your money in a high interest account.

Be serious about it. Keep records showing every purchase as though you had given the order to your stockbroker. Calculate the total cost of the purchase, including broker's commission (about 2 per cent, minimum £10 to £20) and stamp duty (½ per cent). Record your sales in the same way. Do not fool yourself. Remember you must pay commission on a sale too.

Play the game until you feel confident, then tot up how you have done. If you show a good profit then consider playing for real. Also compare how your money would have done in a bank or building society.

Dip one toe in the market. Use only one third of your speculation fund and be prepared to lose some. Regard it as part of your tuition fee. As with many other apsects of life there is no substitute for experience on the stock exchange. But naturally, you should aim to avoid paying too high a price for your experience.

Beware of beginner's luck. You may start in the middle of a raging *bull market*, a time when shares are generally rising in value (more about that later).

While there is no minimum amount needed to enter the stock market (fortunes have been made from an initial stake of £100) in practical terms these days £600 to £1,000 is probably the smallest sum required for each share.

How many different shares should you buy?

The long-term investor should certainly not put all his eggs in one basket, but the speculator, should play for meaningful stakes. After all, if you start with £600 and buy ten different holdings of £60 each spread evenly over the market you are unlikely to pick ten winners. The most likely result is that in a rising bull market you will make a small profit over, say, a three month period, and if a *bear market*, when shares generally fall in value, you will make a small loss. In other words, the winners and losers will cancel each other out. Even if you make a profit the chances of you becoming rich in time to enjoy it are exceedingly rare.

Also, the more shares you hold the more time you must spend monitoring their movements and worrying about them. You can become confused, panicky even, and that could be fatal. You are like a juggler trying to keep too many balls in the air.

The stop-loss system

That is all very well, you may say, but if I buy only one or two different shares and they go down I stand to lose a lot of my stake. The answer is the *stop-loss system*.

This is how it works. When you buy a share you set a price at which you will sell if the price begins to fall instead of rising. For the average share the stop-loss price should be set between 10 per cent and 20 per cent below the price you paid. With actively traded shares in large companies such as Shell and ICI the stop-loss level can be reduced to between 5 and 10 per cent. A share in a smaller company in which dealings are less frequent or a more speculative share in which the price movements are greater would warrant a higher margin, say up to 30 per cent.

As the share price rises so you increase your stop-loss figure. For example, you buy Shell at 800 and fix your stop-loss price at 720 (ie 10 per cent margin). Shell goes up to 900 so your stop-loss price becomes 810.

Sounds simple. If your stop-loss margin is 10 per cent then you cannot lose more than 10 per cent of your stake, plus your stockbroker's charges. But you have to maintain firm control. It is easy to be swayed by other opinions and considerations. *The idea of limiting your loss on a bad venture is the most difficult for some speculators to accept.*

It is not a perfect system either. No system is. Otherwise there would be many more rich people around. Not all shares which drop 10 or 20 per cent go on down. By using this system you may sometimes sell a good share too soon and frustratingly watch it go on up and up. That is the price you pay for operating a safety net.

Stockbrokers in this country do not normally operate automatic stop-loss systems on behalf of their clients. The ordinary speculator must keep an eye on his own shares. The stockbroker will always quote you a price on the telephone and as soon as he has got to know you he will accept an order to buy or sell over the telephone. Fixing the stop-loss price is a test of your experience and skill.

One of the chief exponents of the stop-less system was Nicolas Darvas, a professional dancer, who made a fortune on *Wall Street*, where the New York Stock Exchange is based, without ever going there. He had his own personal technique – but then you will appreciate as you read on that speculating is a very personal business.

Checklist
1. Are you investing or speculating?
2. Set aside sufficient money for your needs before you decide how much to put in your speculation fund.
3. Never borrow to play the market.
4. First play the market without money.
5. Begin slowly and beware of beginner's luck.
6. Decide how many holdings to buy.
7. Practise the stop-loss system.

2

Sorting Out The Bulls From The Bears

Like many other facets of life stock markets move in cycles. When prices are rising it is known as a *bull market* and when they are falling it is called a *bear market*. Similarly, a person who expects prices to rise is a *bull* and one who expects them to fall is a *bear*.

At the beginning of an upswing, share prices react to improving economic conditions. As the improvement gathers strength buyers become more confident and prices rise. Eventually, buyers become over-optimistic, they only see the good news, and many people who never bought shares before are tempted into the market as an easy way of making money.

Too high a price is put on the future and inevitably there is a reaction. Optimism gives way to pessimism and prices fall. After a while the pessimism is overdone and a new bull market begins. This is an over-simplified description of the cycle as you will discover later. *But the bull and bear cycle is the primary factor in making money in the stockmarket.*

Before you enter into any deal you should decide quite definitely whether the market is in a bull or a bear phase. Then go with the market. *Never buck the trend.*

If the market is in an upswing go ahead and buy the share or shares you fancy, but if it is in a downswing do nothing. Keep your money on deposit.

True, it is possible to make money in a falling bear market by various methods such as selling shares you do not have and buying them later when the price has dropped, known technically as *selling short*, but these kind of deals are best left to the professional operator. The small operator is wise to adopt an attitude of masterly inactivity during a bear period.

The trouble is, when you have been in the market for a little while and hopefully made a few pounds, it is not easy to sit on your hands. This is especially so when you see the prices of some of your favourite shares drop by thirty or forty per cent. But learn to be patient and you will reap your reward.

How long does a bull or a bear market last?
Answer: history shows that it can be anything from one to fifteen years. Professor Jevons, who had a theory that sun-spots have some bearing on commerce and the state of minds, believed that the normal time for the full cycle was ten years. His theory seemed to be borne out by the facts for a long period in the last century, but more recent movements have been less regular. The stock market stubbornly refuses to conform to any pattern and just when some bright spark thinks he has found one it goes off in a different direction and makes a fool of him.

To what extent does the market rise or fall during these periods? Answer: it is limited only to the sentiment of the investors. You will have heard of the 1929 Wall Street crash and the panic that ensued. Fortunately, there has been nothing as bad as that since.

However, in January 1974 the Financial Times ordinary share index stood at 339. One year later, January 1975, it had fallen to 146. Yet ten months later, November 1975, it had risen again to 377. Here was a good opportunity to make a killing. All you needed was the courage of your conviction that despite the dark clouds overhead the sun would surely shine again.

The Financial Times Ordinary Share Index which is published every day the market opens, is produced by averaging out the prices of 30 active shares from companies whose share movements are thought to reflect the general movement in the market as a whole. The FT-SE 100 Share Index and the FT-Actuaries All Share Index, monitor a larger number of shares and tend therefore to reflect the mood of the market more accurately.

The $64,000 question is, how do you determine that elusive moment when the market is about to change direction? You can prepare complicated charts. Or you can follow the so-called experts in the newspapers and on the radio. The trouble is that *the main characteristic end of a rising bull market is when the opinions of financial journalists, stockbrokers, chartists and other investment advisers are rampantly bullish*. They believe share prices will continue to rise just that little bit longer.

So, the other alternative is to use your own judgement. Your feel for the market. You know what is going on in the world. Take note of the experts, but why should they be more right than you?

The end of a bull market represents a period when nothing can justify the prices at which shares are changing hands. People buy anything that is going up regardless of the share's earnings or its intrinsic worth. *It is a time of greed and excitement. It seems that everyone has a stock market tip*.

You might think that these conditions would be easy to recognise, but in practice it is harder to spot the end of a bull market than the end of a bear market. You are carried along with the euphoria.

The picture of the final throes of a bear market is in stark contrast: black despair. Company dividends are being reduced and there is talk about this company or that going broke. Shares are selling well below their true worth.

The average investor is tied up with shares he bought in happier times and at a much higher price. Even so the future looks so gloomy that some investors will sell and take big losses. The wise long swing speculator has sold out long ago. Now he has cash in the bank and is ready to step into the market and make a killing.

Changes of direction in the market

You can be fooled by minor movements or corrections in the market. The market does not go straight up in a bull period and straight down in a bear period; there are swings within swings. Often a sudden upsurge in prices will be followed by a fall caused by speculators taking their profits.

As a general rule a bull period is in force if the market falls but then rises within a few days to reach a point higher than its previous high point.

For example, if the FT index drops from 1350 to 1330 but then recovers to 1360, its highest point ever, you can assume that the 'bull is still running', the market will continue to rise. Similarly, if after a rally the market drops to a point lower than its previous low then the bear is still hunting. These minor swings provide money making opportunities for the experienced speculator.

How the winners did it

Gerald M Leob, who made a fortune on Wall Street some 40 years ago, wrote: 'There is no rule about anything in the stock exchange save perhaps the one that *the key to market tops and bottoms or the key to market advances or declines will never work more than once*. The lock, so to speak, is always changed. Therefore, a little horse sense is far more useful than a lot of theory.'

Do not try to be too clever or greedy. You can do very

well if you stay on the bull for a good part of his run and jump off when he gets too excited. Nathan Rothschild, when asked how he made his fortune, replied: 'By selling too soon.'

As for the bear, make sure he has gone before you venture out. In his case it is better to be late and sure than early and doubtful.

Checklist
1. The bull (prices rising) and the bear (prices falling) cycle is the primary factor in making money in the stock market. Never go against the trend.
2. Watch out for minor movements or corrections.
3. The main characteristic of the end of a bull market is when everyone is rampantly bullish, so be prepared to jump off.
4. In a bear market it is better to be late and sure than early and doubtful.

3

How To Pick A Winning Share

How do you choose a winning share? There are over 2,000 shares quoted in the Financial Times and nearly 7,000 listed on the Stock Exchange. It is rather like studying the runners in a horse race – but with a far larger field. First you must learn how to read the form.

This means knowing how to study a company's annual report and balance sheet and understanding the various indexes and ratios quoted in the newspapers and magazines. In other words you need to learn the fundamentals, just as you would any other trade. Skill and inspiration come later.

Many people find analysing a company's records a fascinating business. Computer enthusiasts can have great fun preparing pretty charts showing, for example, price movements and resistance levels, the levels at which prices are not expected to go above or below.

But all these facts and figures will not guarantee you a winner. If success on the stock exchange was simply a matter of research and analysis there would be a lot more rich investors around. Do not fall into the trap of putting all your faith in statistics. Statistics are dead. It is what is going on now and in the future that really matters. The price of a share is based on supply and demand, not on statistics.

Read all about it

Read the industrial as well as the financial news. But if you see that a company has gained an important contract do not rush in and buy its shares. Shares react to good or bad news before it appears in the newspapers. The initial reaction could be exaggerated, or even totally wrong.

Before you buy any share you should discover everything you can about the company – its management, competitors, profits and possibility for growth. A growth share is your main aim. But it is not only you who must think that the share is a winner – other investors must think so too, preferably after you have already bought it.

You may spot a promising growth situation as you go about your day-to-day affairs; a new drug, a fashion house, or a food chain. 'They must be making a bomb' you say to yourself. This may be true and there is no reason why you should not have your share of the profits (provided their shares are available in the market) but you must do your homework first.

All is not what it seems

Many years ago I bought some shares in a company producing pots and pans at very reasonable prices. I liked the product – in fact I bought some myself. The factory was on my way home from work and I noticed that they were working far into the night. I even talked to one of the employees who told me that their order book was full and they were taking on more staff.

I lost more money than I could afford at the time on those shares. The trouble was that they were selling their products too cheaply. A proper study of their annual figures could have given me due warning. I had not done my homework.

Your stockbroker should be able to supply you with

information on the company. He may also be willing to tell you whether he recommends a purchase at the current price, but remember again that no-one has an infallible crystal ball in this game. A stockbroker's opinion, however well informed and considered is no guarantee.

I have missed out on several good deals by listening to my stockbroker. I blame no-one but myself. Have the courage of your own convictions.

The service cards issued by Extel provide another source of information. A typical card gives a summary of the company's reports, profit figures, rights issues and other important events going back over a number of years. Some banks and public libraries subscribe to this service.

In addition to the study of a particular company's affairs you must also consider outside influences. To give a simple example, if car workers are threatening to strike do not buy a share in any company connected with that industry. On the other hand, if a tourist boom is forecast it might persuade you to hang on to your shares in a hotel chain.

Shares move in accordance with supply and demand, but *in the final analysis the value of a share is determined by its return to the investor*. This depends on its profitability and on the value of its assets. Therefore, if you look for undervalued assets you must be on the right track – provided the assets are what people want.

If general conditions are improving ask yourself whether that particular company is having a fair share of the general improvement. Is its value rising? If so, determine whether the price of its shares is low or high with reference to its value. If the price is low buy the shares. Keep it until the price appears to be up to the value and then take your profit.

Some investors study only one or two shares, usually

blue chips such as Shell or ICI. They get to know their intrinsic value and deal mainly in their stocks, buying when they are out of favour and selling when they are riding high. Admittedly, this can be a fairly long-term speculation, but it has proved a reliable one.

Consider these points before you make a purchase
Do not buy an inactive share (i.e. a share in which there are few dealings.) As a speculator you must always be able to sell as soon as you think it is the right moment. Sleep with a lazy dog and you awake with fleas.

Do not buy more of the same shares at a lower price. Once a share starts to fall it often continues on the downward path. A dried up cow goes to the butcher. Average up, never down.

Do not let your political views cloud your judgement. Moral values are a different matter. The Ethical Investment Research and Information Service (EIRIS) set up by Quakers, Methodists, OXFAM and other church organisations provides an ethical analysis of the activities of many companies. Their address is 9, Poland Street, London W1V 3DG.

Do not buy because you are attracted by the name of the company. You may laugh, but many people allow a name to influence their decision.

Be wary of the sure winner. *When you think you have a dead cert, think again.* More people get stung by sure things than by bees.

If the market suddenly rises do not rush to buy. You could be buying at the top price. There is often a reaction to a big rise. Buy on reactions. Sell on sharp rises in price.

Never try to take revenge on the market. This is totally wrong and it could lead you into a reckless gamble. Buy only with a view to making money, not with the idea of making up your losses.

Buy a share in the strongest group

The market does not move as one body. For example, the FT index may rise 50 points in a month, but the shipping and transport group index may actually fall. On the other hand newspaper and publishing shares may rise far above the average. Follow the Leaders and Laggards table in the Financial Times.

If you are playing the business cycle and plan to buy when you think that the bull is just waking up, go for a market leader which responds to an upturn in personal spending (consumer goods) such as Marks and Spencer. Later when the boom gathers strength switch to companies supplying capital goods such as machinery or engineering shares.

Remember, *when* you buy is often more important than *what* you buy. The market is in its strongest position when prices are weak and the outlook gloomy; it is in a weak position when prices are high and business booming. The strong have potential weakness. The weak have potential strength.

Do not buy on the strength of a message from your God. To quote Maurice Baring: 'If you would know what the Lord God thinks of money you only have to look at those to whom he gives it.'

4

Take My Tip

There are plenty of people eager to tell you how to make money out of the stock market; city editors, financial consultants, tip-sheets. They are all experts and they all purport to be in the know. Why not follow their advice and forget about studying company reports and the state of the market?

A few years ago the London Business School carried out a survey on New Year tips given in newspapers such as the Daily Telegraph, the Sunday Times, the Economist and in some well-established tip-sheets. Their verdict was that the tipsters, in general, did slightly better – but only slightly – than if they had used a pin to pick similar sized companies.

Tip sheets

Tip-sheets have enjoyed great popularity for several years now. They contain about eight pages, rarely more, and are published weekly. An annual subscription costs from £40 to £150 although they often make introductory offers. The sheet is sent direct to you through the post.

Some of them have been going for many years. Others have sprung up as interest in the stock market has increased. A good percentage of them disappear after a while, depending on how well their tips work out. They are soon replaced by new stars offering even greater rewards.

Their advertising can be persuasive, showing examples of tips which have risen spectacularly. They do occasionally pick a big winner. The law of averages could have something to do with it. But their losers are forgotten – except, of course, by the poor people who bought them.

The big danger is that they tend to recommend small companies, which have relatively few shares on issue. Remember the advice previously quoted warning the speculator to *steer clear of small inactive shares*.

Tip-sheet editors like shares which have a *thin market* because a small increase in the demand can send the price soaring. They can then say how wonderful they are. Unfortunately, the process can work equally quickly in reverse.

If you do take the advice of a tip-sheet you must move very quickly. Even so, you are unlikely to be quick enough. You are competing with the real professionals. To quote one leading city expert: 'If a share is tipped people are on the telephone by 8.30 on the morning the tip-sheet appears. The share may rise rapidly in the first hour of dealing, but by ten o'clock the game is over.'

There is also the chance that someone involved in the production of the tip-sheet, a printer, distributor, or heaven forbid, a contributor, has already bought the shares and given the game away beforehand. You would then buy right at the top.

Not all tip-sheets are irresponsible. Their tips may well be based on sound arguments, but one must ask the obvious question: if a tip-sheet contributor has a sure thing why does he want to share it with others? Why does he not keep it to himself and make a killing? Such generosity runs against human nature.

'Inside' information
This question of reliability also applies to the chap on the

nineteenth hole of the golf course or in the local pub who got a tip from a friend in the city who really is in the know. Such tips should be scrupulously considered. They could be dangerous. Even assuming there is any foundation in the story it is extremely unlikely that you will be within the first thousand people to hear about it. These stories go round the market like wildfire.

In my early days in the city I had an 'insider' tip. I heard that a certain company had made a greatly increased profit and was going to increase its dividend. The information came straight from the horse's mouth – from a man who had resigned a few days earlier from the financial division of the company.

I bought the shares and waited for the annual report to be announced. Everything I had been told was true. The profits rose and the dividend was increased. I rang my stockbroker anticipating selling at a nice profit. To my dismay the shares had fallen sixpence. The market had anticipated the news weeks before and the smart operators had already taken their profits.

The nature of the market is to discount the future. When the news is out – and the future has become the present – the game is over.

I should have bought those shares two months before the results were due and sold them just before the dividend announcement. I would then have made a profit of over 20 per cent.

After the dividend announcement has been made the question is not how much profits have increased in the past year, but how much more will they increase in the year ahead. This may give you another chance to make money. If the price falls after the dividend announcement so that the shares are standing below value, but in your opinion the future for the company is bright, then this may be the time to get in on the cheap.

An old market maxim runs: 'Where there's a tip

there's a tap.' This means that tips are sometimes started by someone who is anxious to unload a batch of shares in that particular company. Rumour that there is about to be a take-over bid for the company is a favourite ploy.

Never follow a tip blindly. Buy only when you consider the share meets all your criterion for a sensible purchase. Then, if the rumour turns out to be false you are not left holding a dud.

Judy Garland once said: 'I was advised those stocks and shares would make me a lot of money on the side. After ten years all I had on the side was appendicitis.'

5

Getting In First

A lot of people have made money out of new share issues. TSB and British Telecom are the best known examples. The city institutions which offer these shares to the market are keen that the shares should get off to a good start. For this reason they tend to fix the offer price slightly below their estimate of the opening market price. It is a very difficult exercise and it is not surprising that some of these issues are excellent value and become heavily oversubscribed.

The number of new issues, due both to private companies and state owned corporations being sold to the public, has increased considerably over the past few years, and long queues of eager applicants outside the banks which handle the issue have become a common sight.

Stags
Obviously, not all these people are long term investors. Many of them are what the market call *stags*. This is the term for a person who has no intention of holding the shares obtained in a new issue, but to sell them at a premium (an immediate profit) as soon as dealings begin. Stags have become so numerous of late and in some cases their charges so ferocious that the police have been called to keep order. Many speculators have come to regard the game as not worthwhile.

However, you only have to complete the application form and post it off to stand the same chance as anyone else of getting some shares, even though it may be only a small number. The people who form the queues at the last moment are mostly representatives of stockbrokers and other financial institutions depositing applications on behalf of their clients or speculators who have waited to see how the market is behaving and having judged that the issue will go well are prepared to hit it with a large sum.

The market is full of surprises and there is always the danger that sentiment over an issue will change suddenly, possibly at the very last moment. By applying for more shares than you really want, or can afford, you risk getting landed with them and incurring a fearful loss.

The shares are usually advertised for sale in the Financial Times and other newspapers about five days before the closing date. The prospectus for the issue is published together with an application form. Copies of the form can also be obtained from the banks handling the issue.

All applications received by 10am on the closing date are handled, but if the offer is oversubscribed at that time the list is officially closed at one minute past ten.

When an offer is hugely oversubscribed the smaller applications are often subjected to a ballot so that the unlucky investor will not receive any shares. Applicants for a larger number of shares receive a proportion (sometimes a very small one, maybe less than 2 per cent) of the shares they applied for.

In order to curb abuses of the system the issuing house usually warns that multiple applications from the same person will be weeded out and rejected and that all cheques sent with applications will be cleared before any allotment is made. The aim of clearing the cheques is to discourage applicants from writing cheques for a larger amount than their bank account will stand on the presumption that the allotments will be scaled down.

If your application is scaled down to say 200 shares and the shares go up only a modest amount a large percentage of your profit will be taken by stockbrokers' charges when you sell and loss of interest on your stake money (which is normally much more than the shares allocated).

Betting on a certainty

Some issues such as British Telecom, British Gas and the TSB receive wide pre-launch publicity. You can get a fair idea of how these kind of issues will go from reading the newspapers. It would have been a great shock if British Telecom had not been a success and small applicants had not been treated well in support of the concept of wider share ownership. However, these near certainties are comparatively rare.

There are new issues almost every week of the year, but not all of them attract a premium and only a few are worth *stagging* (buying for a quick return). See the recent issues column in the Financial Times.

Nevertheless, if you have confidence in a share you might consider buying some or adding to your allotment after dealings begin. Good shares often rise substantially after they come on the market. British Telecom was a good buy at around 50p premium during the first days of dealings.

Tenders

Another way of putting shares on the market is to issue them for *tender*. This is the same as an issue for sale except that the price of the share is not fixed in advance, although a minimum price is usually stated. You have to give the price at which you are prepared to purchase the number of shares you apply for. Applications are then accepted starting from the highest price offered until the entire issue is taken up.

For example, supposing 500,000 shares are offered at the minimum price of £2 and applications are received as follows:

100,000 shares tendered for at £2.40
100,000 shares tendered for at £2.30
300,000 shares tendered for at £2.20
200,000 shares tendered for at £2.10
200,000 shares tendered for at £2.00

In this case the issue is oversubscribed and the 500,000 shares offered would be allotted at £2.20 per share.

Obviously, *tender* issues offer less scope for the *stags*, but this does not mean that they should be ignored. Most tender issues open slightly above the minimum price. Your best plan is to bid the price you think the shares are worth as a good short-term buy. You will not have to pay more and you may pick up a bargain.

Placing

Small issues of shares which are unlikely to raise much public interest are sometimes *placed* with city institutions or through a stockbroker to his clients. Sometimes these shares reach a high premium and it is worthwhile keeping an eye open for these issues. If you see an issue which attracts you contact your stockbroker quickly.

In offers for sale successful applicants receive *letters of acceptance*. If the shares are not *fully paid*, that is you pay the cost by two or three instalments, the letter will contain a timetable showing the latest dates when further instalments known as *calls* have to be made. It is important to put these dates in your diary as failure to pay an instalment on time may mean that the earlier payments are fortified.

Rights issues

Companies sometimes find it necessary to raise additional

funds for general expansion or special projects. One way of raising the money is to issue new shares to existing shareholders for cash. This is known as a *rights* issue.

Obviously, the shares must be issued at below the current market price or no-one will buy them. However, an issue to the general public on preferential terms would upset existing shareholders so the offer is made to existing holders in proportion to the number of shares they hold eg one for one or one for two.

Shareholders may then decide whether to take up their *rights* by paying for them or selling their *rights* on the market, assuming that there is sufficient demand for them at the time to attract a premium.

A *rights* issue generally depresses the market price of the existing shares, because some shareholders are bound to sell their *rights* either because they simply cannot afford to take them up, or because they do not wish to increase their holding in the company.

Apart from providing a good investment opportunity a *rights* issue can also offer a chance to make a quick profit. A comparatively small rise in the price of the existing shares can mean a big rise in the price of the *rights*. For example, if the existing ordinary shares stand at £3 and the *rights* are issued at £2.80 then one would expect the market price of the *rights nil paid* to be about 20p. Assuming that the ordinary shares make a modest rise to £3.20 it follows that the *rights* would then stand at around 40p. So, a rise of seven per cent in the existing ordinary shares is reflected in a hundred percent rise in the *rights*. Warning: the process works as well in reverse.

6

How To Check The Score

As mentioned in Chapter 3 you need to study the form before you plunge into the market. This means reading the financial section of your newspaper regularly. If you do not buy or have access to the *Financial Times* every day (your local library will keep copies) then you should get a copy at least once a week. I find the Saturday edition the most interesting because it is slanted more towards the personal investor. As for financial magazines there is the weekly *Investor's Chronicle* and several others to choose from.

Before you turn to the news items, the reports of company meetings and the feature articles you need to know how to read the current prices. Here is an example of a share list.

High	Low	Company	Price	+or−	Div	Cover	Yield	P/E
p	p		p	p	p		%	
204	180	J. Sloucher	200	+2	20	2	10	5

The first two columns show the highest and lowest prices the shares have been during the current year. Then comes the name of the company and the price based on the previous day's dealings. It may not be the closing price, because some newspapers set up their lists earlier in the afternoon.

Price

The price quoted is the middle price. There are actually two prices in the market; the buying price and the selling price and the difference between the two represents the dealer's commission. This margin depends largely on the price of the share and how actively it is traded.

For example, the margin on a popular share such as British Telecom standing around 200p would be about 2p, so the broker might quote you 202p to 204p. In other words he can buy for you at 204p and sell at 202p. In this case the newspaper would quote the middle price of 203p.

The next column shows how much the shares went up or down compared with the price quoted on the previous day.

Cover

Then comes the *cover* which shows the extent to which a company's dividend is exceeded by its *earnings* (profits). If a company pays a dividend of 20p a share, but had enough profits to pay 40p a share then the dividend would have been covered twice. The higher the cover the more scope there is for the company to pay out more dividend to its shareholders. Where cover is less than twice you may have reason to suspect that future dividends are in doubt.

Yield

The *yield* is the percentage return a shareholder receives as a dividend on every £100 invested in the company. This is calculated by multiplying the gross dividend by 100 and dividing it by the current share price. For example, if the gross dividend was 20p per share and the share price was 200p the yield would be 10% If the shares rocketed to 400p and the dividend was not increased the yield would fall to 5%. Of course, the lucky investor who was wise enough to buy the shares at 200p would still be getting a 10% yield on his money.

The dividend yield is heavily dependent on the company's pay out policy and is therefore not a very good measure of the company's ranking. Remember too, that as with all types of investment the general rule is the higher the yield the greater the risk.

Price earnings ratio

The last column headed *P/E* refers to the price earnings ratio which is one of the most important yardsticks used to measure the merits of one share against another. It shows how the company is rated in relation to the profits it earns.

It is calculated by taking the current profits (often called earnings) of the company and dividing it by the number of shares issued. For this purpose earnings are defined as profits after tax, less interest payments and dividends to preference shares. This gives an earnings per share figure which is then divided into the current share price to give the P/E ratio. For example, a company with a quoted share price of 200p and earnings of 40p per share would have a P/E ratio of 5.

The figure shows the extent to which the share price is supported by the earnings. The higher the P/E ratio the greater the expectation the market has that profits will rise; buyers normally regard a company with a high P/E ratio as a high flyer and they are therefore willing to pay a comparatively high price for potential future profits. A low P/E ratio indicates that the market regards the company as dull and unlikely to improve its profit record.

The market could have got it wrong and a low P/E may

mean that the share is undervalued and represents a good buy. The skill is to judge whether a share's P/E is over or underrating its potential.

It follows that near the top of a bull market P/E ratios are generally high while at the bottom of a bear market they are low.

7

The Company Report

Companies spend a great deal of money producing glossy annual reports, but few shareholders do more than glance at the pictures and skip through the Chairman's review. Admittedly, the columns of figures look bewildering and the serious investor will need to make a proper study of the subject, but you do not need to be a chartered accountant to gain some useful information from the report and accounts.

The report and accounts are supposed to give a true and fair view of the state of affairs of the company and should the auditors think that this condition has not been met they must say so. Read the auditors' report and if it contains any criticism consider ditching the shares.

Profits
Turning to the accounts, a lot depends on how the net profit figure is calculated. How much has been deducted in the way of *depreciation*, an allowance for the cost of capital assets which will eventually need to be replaced, and other provisions? If this figure is insufficient it could mean that the company appears more profitable than it really is. An explanation can be found in the notes on the accounts which are generally more revealing than the accounts themselves because they give the story behind the bare figures.

Do the current assets, money the company has or is

owed, exceed the current liabilities, money it owes? If not, the company may have difficulty in meeting its immediate bills and that could mean that it has to sell a fixed asset such as a machine or a building in order to pay a current liability. This is not a good sign. Again the notes are important to see how the figures are made up.

If you exclude the stock (eg items which have been manufactured but not yet sold) from the current assets and divide these assets by the current liabilities you get the *quick assets ratio*. This is known as the *acid test* because it indicates how vulnerable the business is to the immediate presentation of all its bills. The traditionally minimum acceptable ratio is 1.1 but the higher the ratio the better. Any figure below 1.0 spells danger for a manufacturing company. Retailers may often fail this test but this is no cause for worry.

Past performance
Whereas the balance sheet shows the financial state of the company on one particular day the statistical summary shows the financial record over the past five years or more. Is the profit growing or falling? A steady growth is best. Violent swings are dangerous.

Are the profits running in roughly the same proportion as the turnover, or better still, increasing? More business without higher profits spells trouble.

The *return on capital employed* shows how profitably the company is being run. If the figure is falling over a period of time and is lower than other companies of the same type, you need to watch out. The ratio is calculated by taking the profit before tax and dividing it by the total of shareholders' funds (share capital plus reserves) plus loans and less any goodwill. To save you the trouble of working this out yourself, many companies quote the ratio in their financial report.

The *net asset value* per share represents the underlying

value of the shares if the assets were sold and divided amongst the shareholders. It is the shareholders' funds less goodwill divided by the number of shares issued. If it is higher than the market value of the shares then the shares are selling at a discount. This does not necessarily mean that they are a bargain. You must consider all the other factors especially the company's prospects in the market place.

Many investors monitor these ratios over a period of time and compare them with other companies. But remember they are merely indicators and a proper assessment of a company is a much more complicated affair.

An item I find of special interest is the number of shares held by the directors. To put it crudely I am encouraged when I see that they are prepared to put their own money where their mouth is. Their holdings and recent changes in such holdings are clearly detailed in the annual report.

The Financial Times, other newspapers and the Investor's Chronicle closely analyse annual reports soon after they are published. A study of such analyses with the actual report alongside will soon put you in the position to understand them yourself. Start off with companies in the high street, that is those you can relate to, and you will be surprised at the amount of detail you can absorb.

8

Formula For Success

Another way to plan your investments is to use a formula plan. Again it must be emphasised that no strategy yet devised is a panacea for all-out success, but formula plans have the virtue of being easy to manage and offer a good chance of above average profits.

The object of the exercise is to *buy cheap* and *sell dear*. Sounds good, doesn't it? But it is not a magic formula for selling at the top of the market and buying at the bottom. You are unlikely to achieve fantastic profits using a formula plan, but you should not suffer severe losses.

Constant £

This is the simplest type of formula plan. You decide in advance how much money you wish to invest in shares, for example £5,000. Then, at regular intervals of, say three months, you calculate the market value of your shares. If the market has risen you sell sufficient shares to reduce your holdings back to your original stake of £5,000 and place the profit on deposit.

If the market has fallen you buy shares to raise the market value of your holdings up to the £5,000, using the money you have on deposit. Of course, if you start the plan at the wrong time and the market falls during the first three months you will need to top up your £5,000 stake.

It is an easy plan to work, but your gains are obviously limited.

Constant ratio

Here you decide in advance what percentage of your investment funds should be in shares, the remainder to be kept on deposit or in fixed interest stock realisable on demand. At predetermined time intervals you then sell or buy shares, regardless of the level of prices, so that the percentage of your stake in equities remains constant.

Let us suppose that you start with an investment fund of £10,000. You decide that you should keep 60 per cent of it i.e. £6,000 in good quality ordinary shares and the remaining 40 per cent i.e. £4,000 in bank and building society accounts.

After six months the stock market has risen so that the total value of your fund is £2,000 more i.e. £12,000. Your shares are now worth £8,000 which is 67 per cent of £12,000. Therefore, you must sell £800 worth of shares to reduce your holdings to £7,200 i.e. 60 per cent of £12,000. You put the £800 (less stockbrokers' charges) into your bank or building society account.

In this way you have taken some of your profits, but kept the remainder in shares for possible further gain. Having increased your fixed income investments you are not so vulnerable to a decline in the market.

Suppose however, that your £10,000 investment fund was set up at just the wrong time and the stock market fell during the next six months. Instead of rising by £2,000 your shares fell by that amount. Your total fund is now worth only £8,000 and your shares £4,000, 50 per cent of £8,000.

Under the constant ratio formula you must now buy £800 more of shares to bring your holding up to £4,800 i.e. 60 per cent of £8,000. You get this money from your bank or building society account.

You must buy the shares no matter how frightened you are that prices will fall further. When you follow a formula plan falling prices provide a chance to buy more shares cheaply to help make up paper losses.

You do not want to change your portfolio, that is all your shares, to restore the predecided share ratio too often otherwise you will cut your profits and run up heavy stockbroker's charges. In practice, therefore some followers of this formula wait until the value of their total fund has increased or decreased by at least 10% before making any move.

Variable ratios
There are more sophisticated formula plans involving variable ratios. In these plans you increase the percentage of shares in your fund as market prices decline and reduce your share holdings as prices rise. For example, if you think the market is near the top of a bull phase you would only be about 10% in shares and 90% in fixed interest. At the bottom of a bear market you would be 90% in shares and 10% in fixed interest.

Of course, you can do better under a variable ratio plan than under a constant plan, but it requires experience and skill to operate successfully.

The more the market swings the better you should do under a formula plan. But it is a long-term plan so do not sink all your money into this kind of venture.

Charts
Stock market charts, whether drawn on paper or on a computer, provide a record of share movements in a convenient form, easier to read than a wealth of information in notebooks and tables.

Basically, the peaks and troughs on a chart represent resistance levels. The top point is where more sellers come in sending the price down and the bottom point is where more buyers are attracted bringing about an upward surge.

There are numerous chart theories and there is no reason why you should not invent some of your own. Can charts really predict the future? If they were always right there would be a lot more millionaires. Supply and demand alone determines how fast, how far and in which direction a share will move. When you consider the many elements, hopes, fears, mass moods, fashions, political chicaneries and world events which mixed together help to set up the supply and demand at any given time, you realise that there is no perfect method of calculating this factor. However, charts can help you to build up a body of experience and knowledge which can be consulted and analysed at any time. Use them as a visual aid to your thinking. But do not put all your faith in the pretty patterns.

Charts of share prices can be obtained from: Investment Research of Cambridge, 28 Panton Street, Cambridge CB2 1DH.

Microcompuer software can be obtained from: Brian Millard Investment Services, 121 High Street, Berkhampstead, Herts. HP4 2DJ.

A book *Bulls, Bears and Microcomputers* by G.T. Childs is available from the Public Affairs Department, The Stock Exchange, EC2N 1HP.

9

When To Sell

When the system you are operating, whether it be formulas, stop-loss, charts, planetary influences or simply intuition convinces you that you should sell a share, then do so – immediately.

Selling is a much more difficult stock market activity than buying. You tend to suffer from hang-ups.

Selling at a loss, for example, is a bitter pill to swallow. Take comfort from the fact that the quick loss is usually the smallest. One of the worst mistakes you can make is to hold on blindly and refuse to admit that you have made a wrong judgment. *Cut your losses quickly.*

A typical beginner's error is to sell a share in which he has made a profit in order to protect a share in which he is making a loss. It is psychologically easier to dispose of a good stock and take a profit than a bad one and take a loss. In general, a share falls because the outlook for it is grim and a share rises because its future looks bright. *Sell a dud, keep a winner.*

Round figure
Another beginner's mistake is to set a round figure as a selling price. Many people are inclined to do this causing a resistance point just below that figure. For example, if you decide to sell a share when it reaches 200p you will probably find that it will rise to around 197p and then fall again, which can be very frustrating. Eventually, it will

fall way down and you will have missed your selling opportunity. *Avoid the round numbers syndrome.*

It can be fatal to form too deep an attachment to a share. You read the glossy company reports and get to know the names of the directors almost as well as the people living down your road.

You follow their efforts to make the company a big success. Maybe they are starting a project in a part of the world of special interest to you or in an activity you know something about. The more you become involved with the company, the more information you receive, the more you tend to ignore the market in general and believe that the share will beat the law of supply and demand. No way. *You do not marry a share when you buy it, nor do you pay alimony on parting.*

Every shopkeeper knows that it is sometimes necessary to hold a clearance sale to get rid of slow moving stock. Look through your portfolio and have a sale now and again.

If a share is slow moving in a rising bull market or has not come up to your expectations after a fair amount of time, sell out. After all, your profits depend to a certain extent on turnover. There may be more exciting opportunities elsewhere.

Some speculators set a time limit and sell if a share has not moved up sufficiently in that period. I prefer a more flexible approach, but you should not let a share idle for too long. *It does not pay to keep dull company.*

Sell in May and go away

This is an old stock market maxim. The market often drops during the early summer and picks up again in the Autumn. Many fund managers and investors are on holiday during this period and as a result there is less activity in the market. People tend to lose interest in the market except for sellers who need the money. Consequently a small amount of selling pressure can send the market down.

Do not sell shares at the wrong time just because it will help reduce your tax bill. However, see A to Z of stock market terms for definition of a bed and breakfast deal.

Bear in mind the maxim *paper profits don't count*. You have not really made a profit until you have turned your shares back into ready cash.

It is better to sell too soon and the shares continue to rise than not sell and see the shares slide, eating away your capital. After all, you then have the money on deposit ready to step into the market again when you see a good opportunity.

One speculator I know regularly looks at each share in his portfolio and asks himself the question: would I buy that share at the current price? If the answer is no he sells it. He believes in always leaving a little profit for the next fellow.

Finally, do not suffer sleepless nights worrying about your shares. If this is happening to you it means that you are over-speculating. *Sell down to your sleeping factor.*

Check List
1. Having made the decision to sell act immediately.
2. Sell a dud, keep a winner.
3. Avoid the round numbers syndrome.
4. Don't fall in love with a share.
5. Don't keep dull company.
6. Remember paper profits don't count.
7. Sell down to your sleeping factor.

10

How To Get A Good Deal
From Your Stockbroker

Before you can take any active part in the stock market you will need the services of a -stockbroker. If you know someone who is getting good service from his stockbroker ask him to arrange an introduction for you. Otherwise, choose one or two from the list at the back of this book. Tell them your needs, roughly how frequently you expect to deal and the amount of money likely to be involved.

For convenience, stockbrokers' services are generally split into three categories:

1. *Dealing only service.* This means that a stockbroker will buy and sell securities for you on a commission basis, but not offer you advice.

2. *Discretionary service.* In this he will consult you about your objectives and tax position and then use his discretion to buy and sell for you while keeping you informed of his actions.

3. *Portfolio advisory service.* Again, after agreeing your investment objectives, he will supply you with advice, information and specific recommendations, but he will only act upon your instructions.

Many brokers distribute a regular investment review to all their clients. It is really a matter of getting to know your stockbroker so that you are able to talk to him on a friendly, but business-like basis. Stockbrokers are keen to have satisfied customers and are generally honest and helpful.

If you live in the country try a stockbroker in your area. Do not be put off if it is only a small firm. Size alone is not a reliable guide. It is the commitment to the private investor which counts. In fact, you may well get a more personal and cheaper service from a local stockbroker than from one of the big city firms who may be more interested in clients with large sums of money to invest.

The small country broker may lack the research facilities of a big city firm, but that need not worry you if you simply want him to buy and sell shares for you at the best rates. In any case he is sure to have access to plenty of financial information. Communicating speedily with the trading floor should be no problem for him either. Try to arrange a meeting at his office, if you can, and have a chat.

Commission

Fixed commission charges disappeared with the Big Bang (see next Chapter for explanation) and competition may drive down the commissions charged to private investors. Shop around for a good deal – you could save yourself a lot of money.

You can deal through your bank, but this is usually more expensive and it could mean a delay in getting your order to the market.

All stockbrokers require a banker's reference and some may ask for a minimum deposit.

Deal only with a stockbroker who is a member of the Stock Exchange. All listed members are strictly supervised and backed by a Compensation Fund in case of any loss to the public through fraud or failure of any member.

You sometimes see firms offering to sell your shares free of commission. These advertisements are usually the work of over-the-counter (OTC) dealers. Although the deals are done free of commission it may well cost you more to deal in this way than through a listed broker. This is because OTC dealers make their own market – they have no access to the trading floor – and their buying and selling prices are rarely as narrow as the prices obtainable in the stock market.

Their advertisements to buy popular new share issues and other such shares from you are usually the beginning of a hard sell to get you to deal in the kind of shares in which they normally trade. These are mostly small or newly formed companies. It is really a venture capital market outside the rules of the stock exchange where there are a few big winners, but many more losers.

You should be even more cautious about dealing with brokers operating from abroad. You sometimes see advertisements in British newspapers offering *free* newsletters. These are a way of discovering names, addresses and telephone numbers and many of these firms are little more than share pushers. Do not be tempted with stories of huge profits. You have no redress if your money disappears.

Clinching the deal

When you give an order to your broker you will have already looked in the morning paper or on a screen service (selected share prices are carried on Prestel, Oracle and Ceefax) and you will know the rough price of the share, though you can ask the broker if he has a more up-to-date price.

You can give your stockbroker an order to deal *at best*, which means he will get the best price he can for you, or preferably a *limit order* stating the maximum price you are prepared to pay or the minimum price at which you are prepared to sell. If you give an *at best* order and the price changes dramatically before the broker is able to clinch the deal he should ring you back and ask you whether you still wish to go ahead. He will also telephone you and report details of the deal or say why he has been unable to make it. Once the deal has been done you cannot go back on it. Your word is your bond.

A contract note confirming the deal should be with you within a few days. Check it and be sure that it is correct in every detail.

In the case of a purchase your name will be recorded in the company's register and a share certificate sent to you, though this may take several weeks. When you sell the shares you must sign a stock transfer form which your stockbroker will send you and pass it with the share certificate to your broker. Your name is then deleted from the register. Of course, there is nothing to stop you selling the shares as soon as you have bought them – you do not have to wait for the certificate.

Keep a record of all your deals and store your share certificates in a safe place.

11

Getting Into Top Gear

When you have gained experience and made some money on the stock market you may decide to be really brave and go for bigger and quicker profits. You can do this by what is known in stock market jargon as gearing.

In financial terms, this works on the same principle as the gears on a bicycle or any other piece of machinery – a small movement at one end makes a larger movement at the other.

There are several ways in which you can jump on to this bandwagon – but beware it can move fast and if you fall off you can get a nasty bump.

Traded options
A *call option* gives you the right to buy a share at a fixed price and within a fixed period. You use it if you think the shares will go up before the option expires.

For example, Lucky Day shares may be standing at 250p in the market. You pay 20p for a three months' call on them. This gives you the option to buy Lucky Day shares at 250p at any time during the next three months.

If the shares rise to 290p, you will make a profit of 20p a share (40p less the 20p you paid for the option). So you will have doubled your money – your outlay is 20p for the option (not 250p the price of the shares).

But if the share price stays at 250p or falls below this

figure, the option will be worthless, and you will have lost all your money.

How does this compare with the ordinary investor, who buys Lucky Day shares at the market price? If he pays 250p for them and they rise to 290p, he will make 40p per share, but on a much larger stake. Far from doubling his original investment, he will make a mere 16%.

If the shares show another 20p rise, he will have increased his investment by 24%. But the lucky option holder would have trebled his money.

Moreover, if the shares fall badly, the option holder cannot lose more than his original stake – which in this case is 20p per share.

On the other hand the investor who buys the actual shares could lose considerably more on each share – though he is unlikely to lose all his money.

Before you become too enthusiastic however, be warned that this is an extremely volatile and sophisticated market. There is a substantial gambling aspect within it. Just as gamblers on coffee and tea futures are not interested in coffee or tea (except for a cup full now and again to steady their nerves) and would be upset if a lorry started unloading tea chests outside their office, so buyers and sellers of options are interested only in the price of the options and not in the related shares. *Most options contracts are never exercised, but are sold before the expiry date*.

The investor has the choice of several *striking* prices, all with their relative premium prices.

In the case of our example share, Lucky Day, the striking prices might be 230, 250 and 270. You stand to make more money if you go for the highest price, simply because the option price is lower. But you are taking a greater risk, because if the shares do not reach that figure, your option will be valueless.

Example of traded option prices

Share	Option price	Cost of option		
		March	June	Sept
	p	p	p	p
Lucky Day	230	26	36	45
(current	250	8	20	28
price 250)	270	3	10	16

Options are dealt with in units called contracts, each of which usually represents 1,000 shares. A buyer of 10 contracts would therefore be dealing in 10,000 shares.

You also have a choice of expiry dates, set at three, six or nine-month intervals into the future.

There are also *put* options which work in reverse and give you the right to sell shares. But anyone buying a put option must have very strong nerves. It is not so easy to become a jeremiah – most people are naturally optimistic.

Besides, your profit is limited with a put option because a share cannot fall below zero. Also, most shares in which options are traded are from large companies which are unlikely to become completely worthless.

A traded option can be bought or sold through a stockbroker at any time before its expiry date, after which it is worthless. Stockbrokers' charges can be high and they are not keen to deal in single 1,000 share lots.

It is essential to study this market for some time before parting with your money. Prices on the London Traded Options Market are quoted in the Financial Times.

Useful literature on the subject can be obtained from Options Development Group, The Stock Exchange, Old Broad Street, London EC2N 1HP.

Warrants

Share warrants are similar to options in so far as they give a right to buy the shares at a future date without an obligation to do so. They offer a future interest in a share for a relatively small investment.

However, they are issued by the company and it is the company and not another investor who delivers the actual shares (in the form of newly issued shares) – when the warrant is exercised.

Share warrants have a much longer life than share options, ranging from three to ten years or longer with an average of around six years. But like ordinary shares they can be traded on the Stock Exchange.

Gearing is the main attraction. But remember, this can work in reverse in a falling market with the result that prices fall further and faster than those of the underlying ordinary shares.

Only a few large companies have issued share warrants; they are more popular with investment trust companies.

The spread between the buying and the selling rate can be high and you need to employ a stockbroker with specialist knowledge of the market.

Nil and partly paid shares
New share offers and rights issues often come on the market in nil or partly paid form. How the effects of gearing can make these a good investment opportunity is explained on page 36.

12

How To Drive A Convertible

Buying a *convertible loan stock* is the closest you can get to to an each-way bet on the stock market.

The convertible is a form of loan stock paying a fixed rate of interest, but with the option to convert into ordinary shares on a specified date or between specified dates.

For example, supposing you pay £100 XYZ convertible loan stock 10% 1996. This will give you a regular 10% interest a year, but with the opportunity to convert into ordinary shares in the company at the rate of three ordinary shares for each £1 stock held on June 1, 1992.

If by 1992 the ordinary shares have risen to, say, £1 each it will obviously pay you to convert and you will have trebled your investment.

On the other hand if the ordinary shares have fallen you can keep the stock and receive the regular 10% yearly interest until the redemption date, 1996. The company will then buy back the stock at the original issue price of £100.

You do not necessarily have to hang on to the stock until the conversion date to make a profit. The price of the convertible moves in line with the price of the ordinary shares, based on the underlying value of the terms of the conversion. But the movement is more moderate in each direction.

Because of its defensive qualities, (because it falls less when prices fall) the price of a company's convertible stock is normally higher than that of its ordinary shares at the time you buy.

Taking the earlier example, let us assume that XYZ ordinary shares are standing at 25p each today. For every £1 you invest, you could buy either four ordinary shares or £1 convertible stock. Remember, the latter is exchangeable for three ordinary shares in 1992. You are therefore effectively paying a 25p extra for the company's convertible stock; this is called a *premium*.

This premium is often quoted in percentage terms. It is calculated by taking the difference between the conversion price and the current share price and dividing it by that share price. In our example the conversion price is 33.3p and the current share price is 25p which gives a premium of 33%.

Obviously, you stand to make more money by buying the ordinary shares, but they are riskier. If their price tumbles you are not protected by the high-interest yield or the chance to get the original issue price back in 1996, as you are with the convertible.

Of course, you are unlikely to get in on the ground floor and buy a convertible at its issue price as in our example. If you pay say £120 for £100 XYZ convertible stock you will only get £100 back in 1996.

The attraction of convertible stock is that it provides you with a comparatively high interest yield – normally far in excess of the ordinary shares – and at the same time offers the chance of capital growth.

The best way to choose a convertible stock is to concentrate on the underlying shares. Pick a company you like and then check whether it has issued any convertible stock. Never buy a convertible in a company you are not enthusiastic about simply because the stock offers a high yield.

Dealing costs are about the same as for ordinary shares and the spread (the difference between the buying and the selling price) is little different from that on the equivalent ordinary shares.

Details of the stocks are given on Extel cards and in the Stock Exchange Investment List, published by Mathieson and Sons (tel: 01-403 5742). Prices of the larger issues are printed in some newspapers. For conversion advice and estimates of potential dividend increases on the underlying shares contact your stockbroker.

Convertible preference shares

There are also a few convertible preference shares on the market. The main difference between these and convertible loan stock is that convertible preference shares are not redeemable at the end of their lives. If you keep them until the last date your only option is to convert them into ordinary shares; you cannot get the issue price back.

Bargain hunters

A share price will rocket and investors may sometimes forget about the convertible. So, instead of a premium the convertible is obtainable at a discount, providing a cheap way into the ordinary shares. It does not happen often and you have to be very quick to snap up such a bargain.

13

Fixed Interest

Most people buy a fixed interest security for the income it provides and the guaranteed capital sum payable at the end of its term.

During the life of the stock however, it can be traded on the Stock Exchange and its price will vary according to supply and demand giving you the chance to make a capital profit. This does not apply to National Savings and Local Authority Loans which are not tradeable.

Gilt-edged

These stocks are issued and guaranteed by the British Government, so there is no question of the dividend not being paid or the funds not being available when the stock matures. A company may go bust, but should the Government get into financial trouble it simply raises taxes or sells an asset.

The many different gilt stocks available are divided into three groups according to their maturity dates. *Shorts* are gilts with less than five years to run before redemption, *mediums* have five to 15 years to run, and the remainder are called *longs*. Then there are a few gilts such as 4% Consols and 3% War Stock which have no maturity dates.

The names given to the stocks such as *Treasury*,

Exchequer, *Funding*, *Consols* are irrelevant to the investor. The important factors are the rate of interest, the length of time before redemption and the current market price.

The current market price of a gilt is determined mainly by the general level of interest rates. If interest rates are low then many gilts stand at a *premium*, ie a price higher than the redemption price. If interest rates are high the price stand at a *discount*, ie a price lower than the redemption price.

But remember, the stock market is always looking to the future. If the market thinks that we are in for an inflationary period and interest rates will be higher when the gilt matures then it will not be considered a good investment and may stand at a discount.

To trade in gilts you must take a view of the future movement of interest rates and back your judgement. The prices of the longer dated gilts usually fluctuate the most because the shorter dated issues tend to move towards their *par* (redemption) value as the redemption date draws near. However, a sudden fall in interest rates could see a sharp rise in the price of short-dated gilts. You must make a thorough study of the market before you start trading.

Some investors use gilts as a means of reducing their tax bills. They buy stock giving a low rate of interest which is taxable, but offers substantial capital appreciation which is not taxable.

Interest yield

If 13½% Exchequer Stock 1994 is standing at 120 you will pay £120 for each £100's worth of stock. Because you have paid £20 more than the par (redemption) value of the stock you will obviously not receive 13½% interest per annum on your investment, but effectively only 11¼%. This figure is known as the interest yield.

Redemption yield

To carry the point a stage further if you keep the stock until its redemption date in 1994 and collect the £100 due your total return, in capital and income terms, will only be 9.37%. This figure is known as the redemption yield.

Index-linked

With a long-term investment of gilts there is always the danger that your capital will be severely diminished by inflation. Hence, the introduction in 1982 of index-linked stocks in which both capital and income are increased in accordance with the Retail Prices Index. The interest yield of these stocks above inflation is around 2%.

How to buy

You can deal in gilt-edged stock through your stockbroker. Generally, the commission charged is slightly less than for equities, although the minimum charge of £15 or £20 for small amounts usually applies.

Alternatively, you can get an application form from your local post office for a minimum charge of £1. The disadvantage is that you will not receive details of the transaction for about three days.

Other fixed interest stocks

Stocks issued by companies bear the added risk that the company may go bust and be unable to pay out when the loan matures. The market price is therefore influenced by the standing of the company as well as interest rates in general.

Check List
1. Before attempting to trade in gilts or other fixed interest securities it is essential to make a thorough study of the market.
2. If you are thinking of buying a gilt as an investment get expert advice. The right gilt for you depends very much on your individual circumstances eg your tax position and when you want your money back.

14

Safety Tips

It is important to keep your share certificates in a safe place and to record all your deals in an investment ledger.

If a share certificate is lost, stolen or accidentally destroyed you will continue to receive any dividends due on the investment, because your holding is registered in the books of the company and cannot be removed without a transfer form signed by you. The difficulty arises when you want to sell the shares or offer them as security for a loan. Then you must produce the certificate.

The company will only issue a duplicate certificate against an indemnity signed by you and countersigned by a bank or an insurance company. Your stockbroker may be able to deal with the problem through a block insurance policy, but whatever way you obtain a duplicate certificate it will involve a fee and you will remain liable to the company for any loss arising as a result of the issue of the duplicate certificate. Unless the original certificate is found you will remain liable ad infinitum.

Allotment letters
A missing renounceable allotment letter is more dangerous. Should you lose this piece of paper tell the bank which dealt with the issue immediately, either by

contacting them direct or through your own bank. A thief could forge your signature on the back of the document and make it marketable – although he would have to do this before the latest date for registration of the renunciation.

Never sign the form of renunciation on the back of the allotment letter until you are ready to post the letter to your stockbroker to meet a sale.

Remember to diarise the dates by which any instalments have to be paid. Failure to pay an instalment can cost you dear. Make a note to send your cheque a few days before the deadline.

Safe in the bank
You can, if you wish, let your bank keep your share certificates in safe custody. The bank will deliver and receive certificates to and from your stockbroker in accordance with your instructions.

If you don't want to be bothered paying in dividends to your bank account, ask your bank for dividend mandate forms for all your shares. The company sends the dividend direct to your bank account and your bank will send you all the tax vouchers at the end of the tax year if you want them.

Or, if you want to be entirely free from paperwork, you could transfer your holdings into the name of your bank's nominee company. The bank will then collect the dividends and credit them to your account, deal with any rights and bonus issues, pay the instalments on allotment letters when due and generally look after your interests. This service is particularly useful if you live abroad or spend long periods away from home.

Dealing
When telephoning an order to buy make sure that you give the exact number and description of the shares. Also

see that your stockbroker has the correct name and address in which the shares are to be registered and check the details on the share certificate when you receive it.

Before selling it is adviseable to check the number of shares you hold with the actual certificate. If you sell more than you hold you will have to buy more in the market to meet your commitment.

Of course, there is no need to delay a sale because you have not yet received the relative certificate. But check your holding with your bought contract note.

Settlement days

The London Stock Exchange settles its bargains at fixed intervals. The year is divided into periods known as account periods. These mostly last a fortnight, though there are a few three-week accounts covering the public holidays.

You should send your cheque in payment so that it is with your stockbroker three days before the settlement date stated on the contract note. If you buy and sell in the same account period you need only settle the balance due.

If you are clever enough to buy and sell the same share within an account period you will save yourself the stamp duty.

You can also deal for *new time*. This means that during the last two days of an account it is possible to deal for the following stock exchange account though you may have to pay slightly more for the shares. If you think the shares are going to make a sudden surge you may consider it worth it.

Gilt-edged stocks and allotment letters are settled immediately. The contract note will read "settlement cash". So, when you buy this stock you must make sure that you have the money readily available.

15

Calling In The Professionals

If you do not have the confidence or do not want the trouble of building your own portfolio of shares you can still make money on the Stock Exchange.

You can use the services of the professionals by investing in unit trusts, insurance bonds (linked to unit trusts) or investment trusts – or a mixture of all three. These investments have the advantage that your money is spread over a large number of companies, thus reducing the risks.

Unit trusts
A unit trust is a trust fund held on behalf of the investors by the trustees. The trustees are often banks, insurance companies or large financial institutions.

You should not draw too much comfort from the big names, thinking that they will never do anything rash and your money is absolutely safe. The trustees simply act as custodians, looking after the cash and securities and ensuring that the provisions of the trust deed are adhered to.

The pool of investors' funds is dealt with by the fund managers who use the money to buy and sell shares as they think fit. It is their overall performance that should concern you.

Choosing a trust

There are over 1,000 unit trusts in the UK, ranging from general trusts with a wide spread of investments to specialised trusts concentrating on sections of the market such as small companies, special situations, fixed interest, or on certain areas of the world.

Do not be easily swayed by the advertisements. It is amazing the number of people who complete the application forms in newspapers for unit trusts and send off their cheque, often for thousands of pounds, without going into the matter more deeply. They would not dream of spending that kind of money so rashly on anything else.

Be sure that the investment fits in with your overall financial strategy. Check the long-term investment record of that particular management. League tables are published in magazines such as *Money Management* (monthly) and *Investment Adviser* (weekly). The theory is that a manager who has done well in the past will do well in the future. But check that the management has not changed.

As with all successful investment, timing is important. Because the trusts are investing in the stock market they are subject to its bull and bear phases. Obviously, the manager will sell shares and hold the cash in the fund if he thinks that a bear market is near. He has a research department to help him make this and individual investment decisions. But he can still be wrong. The warning on all unit trust advertisements that your units can go down as well as up is for real.

The price of a unit, ignoring the management charges, represents in simple terms the value of the shares and any cash held in the fund divided by the number of units in circulation.

There is a fixed charge, normally 5%, when you buy the units. This accounts for the difference between the buying (offer price) and the selling (bid price) of the units. Discounts are sometimes offered, especially with new issues.

A management fee, usually between 1% and 1¼% of the value of the trust portfolio is also levied each year. This is deducted directly from the trust fund and is reflected in the price of the units.

Trading

Though unit trusts are generally regarded as long-term investments there is nothing to stop you trading in them. The specialist trusts fluctuate most highly and will therefore be the greatest interest to you.

There is plenty of advice available in the financial pages of newspapers and magazines – though much of it may be contradictory. It is rare for one trust to stay top of the league for more than a year.

A strategy which has paid off for some investors is to buy a trust which has performed badly over the past year. It often does better the following year. Then the investor sells and reinvests in another bad performer. But stick to long-term good performing groups.

Another strategy is to buy units in a trust which has just become a top performance on the basis that it still has some way to go.

If you plan to switch frequently between trusts in the same management group you should be able to avoid paying full initial charge and have it reduced from 5% to 3%, 2% or even 1%.

For more information about unit trusts, write to the Unit Trust Association, Park House, 16 Finsbury Circus, London EC2M 7SP. Tel: 01-638 3071.

Insurance Bonds

This is a single premium life insurance policy based on unit trusts or funds. The insurance content of the policy usually consists of a guaranteed minimum sum payable if you die, but the main emphasis of the policy is on investment.

Your investment is linked to one or more of the management group's funds with the advantage that you can switch between different types of funds (eg deposit, property, unit trust linked), for a nominal fee of a few pounds, compared with the 5% it costs to switch out of unit trusts. With some bonds you are allowed one switch a year free.

There are tax disadvantages however, particularly for standard tax payers. Capital gains tax must be paid by the insurance company on the bond whereas unit trusts are exempt. For this reason bonds almost always perform worse than unit trusts.

Managed bonds

Most management groups offer a managed bond through an insurance company which consists of investments in their various specific funds. This investment mix is monitored regularly and the proportions changed at the managers' discretion.

This is not to be confused with a *broker managed bond* when an independent insurance broker switches between funds within a particular management group on your behalf. There is no reason to think an insurance broker will be more skillful than an investment manager.

There are also *managed unit trust portfolios* which are unit trusts invested in other unit trusts from the same management group. The managers switch between trusts for you without you incurring charges.

Going off-shore

Unit trusts and insurance bonds based in tax havens such as Jersey, Isle of Man or the Cayman Islands are more tax efficient for the non-resident of the UK. The advantages

to a UK resident is small and management expenses tend
to be on the high side.

Although the major British institutions who look after
some of these funds are perfectly sound this does not
apply to all off-shore operators. Get tax advice and then
think again before placing your money outside the care of
the UK investor protection.

Investment trusts

An investment trust is similar to a unit trust in so far as it
is managed by professionals who invest its funds in the
shares of many companies.

The difference is that an investment trust is a company
in its own right. Its shares are bought and sold on the
Stock Exchange and their price fluctuates, as all shares
do, in accordance with supply and demand.

Shares in an investment trust are generally at a
discount to its underlying assets. Sounds like a bargain,
doesn't it? It is not quite as simple as that but, in fact,
investment trusts often perform better than unit trusts
over a long period.

You pay stockbroker's commission at the usual rate
when you buy, but the management charges are generally
well below those of unit trusts.

Statistics showing the past performance of trusts can
be obtained from the Association of Investment Trust
Companies who also publish a useful free booklet entitled
More for your Money. Their address is Park House, 16
Finsbury Circus, London EC2M 7JJ. Tel: 01-588 5347.

16

Personal Equity Plan

If you wish to make a long-term investment in shares rather than a speculation you should consider a Personal Equity Plan. The aim is to attract·small investors into buying shares, unit trusts and investment trusts by giving them the following tax reliefs:

1. If you reinvest the dividends you receive you will not be liable to income tax on them.
2. Any profit you make when you sell the shares will not be liable for capital gains tax.

To qualify for these concessions you must keep your money invested for a full calender year. So if you invest before 31 December 1987 you will have to keep the investments until 1 January 1989 to record a full calender year.

You must invest through a PEP manager – most are unit trust groups, banks, insurance companies, stock-brokers or building societies, but you will be the beneficial owner of the shares.

The most you can invest is a lump sum of £2,400 a year or £200 a month. A maximum of £420 or 25% of the total invested, whichever is the higher, can be held in unit trusts and/or investment trusts and the rest must be in ordinary shares in UK incorporated companies. It is possible these limits will be changed in the 1988 Budget.

You can take out a new plan each year, if you wish with different managers, but you are allowed only one plan a year. You can switch managers at any time.

Plan managers, on behalf of subscribers, can switch investments without any capital gains tax, provided the proceeds of the sales are reinvested within 28 days. They must also reinvest any dividends in order to gain tax relief, but they can keep up to 10% of the value of the fund in cash.

Although the yearly investment allowance is small, over a long-term of say five years, the investments could give a good return, especially when you take into account the useful tax benefits.

The scheme is not available in Ireland.

17

A to Z of Stock Market Words

Account The Stock Exchange calendar is divided into a series of accounts. Most of them are two weeks long from Monday to the Friday week. A few last three weeks, especially when a Bank Holiday falls within the period. All deals carried out within an account period have to be paid for ten days after the last day of the account. This day is known as settlement day.

Account trading If you buy and sell the same holding of shares during an account period you pay only the net loss or receive only the net profit on the deal. No stamp duty is payable on such deals. See Closing deal.

After hours deal The stock exchange closes at 3.30pm but deals are often done after this time and the transaction dated the following day.

Allotment letter A document showing that you have been allotted a certain number of newly issued shares.

All share index See FT-Actuaries All-Share Index.

Annual general meeting (AGM) Every company must have an AGM each year, to allow shareholders to vote on the accounts, directors and dividends and question the board on the company's affairs.

Annual Report The yearly independently audited report to shareholders which must be produced by all publicly quoted companies.

Articles of Association A document setting out the objects and administration of the company.

At best An order to a stockbroker to get the best possible price he can obtain for your benefit as opposed to limiting your order to a fixed price.

Balance sheet A statement of assets and liabilities that must form part of a company's accounts.

Bargain The term for any deal on the stock exchange, purchase or sale.

Bear Someone who thinks that the price of a share or stock market prices in general are about to fall.

Bearer stocks Stocks which are not registered in the name of the owner. They are therefore transferable by delivery like a currency note and should always be kept in a safe place, preferably in the bank.

Bed and breakfast deal Selling shares one day and buying them back the next in order to establish a profit or a loss for tax purposes.

Bid price The price you sell your stocks or shares.

Big bang New Stock Exchange regulations with effect from 27th October 1986. Briefly, it means the end of the closed shop whereby stockbrokers could only deal with jobbers (the market wholesalers of shares). Now all Stock Exchange firms can combine the job of stockbroker and jobber in which case they will be known as market-makers. Jobbers are finished. Also the minimum commission on share deals is abolished.

Information technology will expand. A market-maker will be able to display his current prices on terminals accessible anywhere in Britain – and indeed the world. Deals must be reported to a central computer within five minutes by the market-maker. You will not only be able to tell what the latest prices are, but also the volume of business being done.

Blue button A stockbroker's clerk who is allowed on the trading floor.

Blue chip The shares of large well established companies. The expression is thought to have been derived from blue chips, the highest denomination of chips used in casinos.

Bonus issue A free issue of shares to shareholders in proportion to their existing holdings. For example, if you hold 200 shares in Lucky Days PLC who give a bonus issue of one for one you will receive another 200 shares. You now hold 400 shares, but you may be no better off initially because the price of the shares in the market can halve. The object of the exercise is to divide the company's capital into more manageable units. Also known as scrip issue or capitalisation issue.

Bull Someone who thinks that the price of a share or the market in general is about to rise.

Business expansion scheme A scheme for allowing investors to put money into shares which are not quoted at the stock exchange or the Unlisted Securities Market. Buyers get tax relief if they hold the shares for at least five years. The aim is to help small companies obtain finance.

Call A further instalment due on shares which are only partly paid. For example, there were two calls on British Telecom shares of 40p each.

Call option See options.

Capital The money used to set up a business. **Share capital** is the money which is raised by selling ordinary and preference shares to shareholders. **Loan capital** is long-term borrowings. **Authorised capital** is the total amount in shares a company is empowered to issue. **Paid-up capital** is the amount of shares the company has sold to shareholders.

Capitalisation issue See Bonus issue. Also known as scrip issue.

Cash settlement Some deals such as gilts and traded options are done for cash rather than for account settlement. These deals have to be settled the day following the deal.

Closing A deal which reverses one done earlier in the same stock exchange account. No stamp duty is payable on such deals.

Compensation fund A fund maintained by the Stock Exchange to make good any losses to the public if a stockbroker should fail.

Convertible stock A form of loan stock convertible into ordinary shares usually on a specified date, or between specified dates. For example, a convertible loan stock 9%

1992 pays a regular 9% interest a year, but you have the choice to convert it into ordinary shares in the company at a specified rate of exchange (e.g. 2 ordinary shares for each £1 of loan stock) on say 1st June 1992. In some cases you are given a choice of dates and rates of exchange. For example, a convertible loan stock 1992/4 could offer you the choice of converting to ordinary shares on 1st June 1992 at 10 ordinary shares per £1 stock, or 1st June 1994 at 8 ordinary shares per £1 stock.

It can be said that convertible stock offers a two-way bet because you continue to receive regular interest, but if the ordinary shares go up so will the price of the stock in accordance with the underlying value of the terms of the conversion. On the other hand, if the ordinary shares fall you can keep the convertible stock until its redemption date and continue to receive the regular interest payments.

Contract note A written confirmation from the broker that a bargain (buying or selling) has been carried out.

Coupon is the amount of interest payable on a fixed interest stock.

Cum dividend Shares sold entitling the buyer to receive the next dividend.

Cum rights A share bought together with the rights issue attached to it.

Cum scrip A share bought together with the scrip issue attached to it.

Dawn raid The purchase of a large number of shares early in the morning at the opening of the market. Often the first step in a takeover bid.

Dealing Buying and selling shares.

Dealing for new time During the last two days of an account it is possible to deal for the following stock exchange account. Settlement date will then be the one applying to the next account.

Debenture Stock issued by a company and backed by its assets. It carries a fixed interest rate and is quoted like Government stock in terms of £100 nominal units. Its market value will move in sympathy with interest rates.

Depreciation Money set aside to pay for the replacement of assets.

Dividend The part of a company's profits distributed to shareholders, usually on a regular basis. An interim dividend is paid at the half-year stage and a final dividend at the end of the full year.

Dividend cover The number of times the gross dividend could have been paid from the company's profits (after tax and payment of interest and preference share dividends).

Earnings per share A company's profits (after payment of interest and preference share dividends) dividend by the number of shares issued.

Equities Ordinary shares as distinct from debenture and loan stock. If the company does badly the dividend to ordinary shareholders is the first to be cut, but if the company does well the ordinary shareholder can expect to receive an increased dividend. The ordinary shareholder takes the greater risk in the expectation of receiving the greater reward.

Ex-dividend A share bought without the right to receive the next dividend which is retained by the seller.

Ex-rights A share bought ex-rights is not entitled to receive the rights issue previously attached to it.

Ex-scrip A share bought ex-scrip excludes the rights to the scrip issue attached to it.

Extraordinary general meeting A special meeting called to provide shareholders with an opportunity to consider some special decision or happening concerning the company.

Final The dividend declared with a company's year-end results.

Flotation When a company's shares are offered on the market for the first time.

FT-SE 100 The Financial Times Stock Exchange 100 Share Index (Footsie). The index is recalculated every minute and is considered by many to be the best barometer of the market.

FT Ordinary Share Index Probably the most quoted of the three FT indexes. Also known as the 30 Share Index.

FT-Actuaries All-Share Index Index covering 734 shares. A slightly misleading title.

Futures Contracts which give the holder the right to buy or sell the FT-SE 100 Share Index for an agreed price at a future date.

Gilts An abbreviation for gilt-edged. Stock issued

issued by the Government on which there is little risk of default and an annual fixed rate of return.

Gross Interest paid without deduction of tax.

Hammering The expulsion of a member of the stock exchange because he is unable to meet his commitments.

Hedge A means of insuring the risk.

Index linked gilt Government stock with interest and final redemption payment tied to the Retail Price Index.

Institutions A term used to cover all the insurance companies, banks, building societies, unit trusts, investment trusts, pension funds and similar large investment organisations. Institutional buying or support is sometimes given as a reason for a share's rise.

Investment club A club where people meet to talk about investments and to capitalise on the skills and knowledge of the members. If you are interested in joining one of these clubs contact the National Association of Investment Clubs, Halifax House, 5, Fenwick Street, Liverpool L12 0PR.

Investment Trust A company which invests in shares. It differs from a unit trust because its own shares are quoted on the stock exchange. To discover more about Investment Trusts contact the Association of Investment Trust Companies, Park House (6th Floor), 16 Finsbury Circus, London EC2M 7JJ.

Jobber Someone who deals in shares for a broker, but his function ceased on 27th October 1986. See Big Bang.

Limit order An order to a stockbroker specifying a price limit so that the deal can only be done at that price or better.

Liquidation The conversion of assets into cash.

Listed company A company whose shares have been listed and are dealt on the Stock Exchange.

Loan stock Stock bearing a fixed rate of interest. Unlike debenture stock it need not be secured by assets.

Long Someone holding shares can be said to be long of them.

Longs When used in connection with stocks it refers to long-dated stocks with maturity dates of fifteen years and more.

Market-maker New name for a broker who fixes the price of stocks and shares.

Medium term Refers to stock with maturity dates of five to fifteen years.

Middle price Halfway between the bid and offer price.

Net asset value The value of a company after all debts have been paid expressed in pence per share.

New issue A company coming to the market for the first time.

New time See dealing for new time.

Nominee Someone acting on another's behalf. Shares

may be registered in the name of a nominee rather than in your own name to allow the nominee to manage them for you (i.e. deal with rights issues etc.). This service can be very useful if you live abroad or are often away from home. Banks sometimes insist that you transfer your shares into the name of their nominee company if you offer them as security for a loan. The bank is then able to sell the shares if you fail to repay the loan.

Nominal value The face value of a share or stock as opposed to its market value, also called par value.

Offer price The price at which you can buy stocks and shares.

Options The right to buy (**call option**) or sell (**put option**) a specified share at a specified price within a specified period. For this privilege you pay **option money**. There is no obligation for you to buy or sell the shares. You can let the option lapse if you wish. Example: You pay 20p per share for a three months' call option on Lucky Day shares at 265p, being the price at which they are standing in the market at present. During the next three months the shares rise to 305p so you take up your option to buy at 265p and make a net profit of around 20p a share. Alternatively, if the shares fall to 250p you do not take up your option, but lose 20p per share.

A *double option* gives the right to buy or sell a share. A *traded option* is an option which itself can be traded throughout the course of its life.

Traded option prices are quoted in the *Financial Times*. For further information and literature contact the Options Development Group, The Stock Exchange, London EC2N 1HP.

The main attraction of options is that you limit your

risks but not your rewards. The rule is if you see a good profit, take it quickly. Do not play with options unless you can lose your entire option premium and still afford a holiday on the French Riviera.

Ordinary share A share on which the dividends vary in amount depending on the decision of the directors and based on the profitability of the company.

Over the counter market (OTC) A market outside the stock exchange in which small companies are able to raise money by issuing shares to the public. Very risky.

Par The nominal value of a stock or share.

Partly paid Shares which have been only partly paid for and on which further payment or payments are due.

Penny shares Shares with a market value of less than 10p to 50p.

Plc Public Limited Company (previously Ltd). Private limited companies are still Ltd so you can now tell the difference. Some Plc companies are not quoted on the Stock Exchange.

Placing The sale of a large number of shares in one company by arrangement direct to institutions and others without going through the market.

Portfolio A selection of shares held by an individual or a fund.

Preference share A share giving a fixed rate of dividend. The dividend ranks ahead of ordinary shares, but below debentures and loan stock.

Price-earnings ratio (P/E) This is calculated by taking

the current earnings (profits after certain deductions) of the company and dividing them by the number of shares issued. This gives the earnings by share figure. It is then divided into the current share price which gives the P/E ratio. See also Earnings per share.

Prospectus An independently audited document detailing a company's financial history and current situation and published ahead of a new share issue.

Proxy Someone who votes on your behalf if you cannot attend a shareholders' meeting. You can tell your proxy how to vote or let him make up his own mind.

Quoted A share listed on the stock exchange.

Redemption The date when the nominal value of a stock will be repaid to the holder.

Redemption yield The yearly return you get from a fixed interest stock which you hold until it is redeemed. It consists of two parts: the interest, often after tax, and the averaged out difference between what you paid and the value at redemption.

Registered stock Stock in which the name of the holder is listed in the company's register and the stock is transferable only by his signature on a stock transfer form as opposed to bearer stock which is transferable by delivery.

Renunciation The giving up of the right to be registered as the holder of a new issue, enabling the issue to be transferred to another.

Rights issue The issue of extra shares to existing shareholders, usually at a preferential price.

Scrip issue Same as Bonus issue.

Settlement day The day on which all deals for a stock exchange account period must be settled.

Securities A general term for stocks and shares.

Share certificate An official document issued by the company stating the name of the shareholder and the number of shares owned.

Share perks A number of companies give benefits to their shareholders. These include discounts on wine, clothes, holidays, dry-cleaning and light fittings.

Short If you sell a stock which you do not own you are said to be selling short.

Shorts Government stock due for repayment within five years.

Spread The difference between the buying and the selling price. Or a variety of investments.

Stag Someone who applies for shares in a new issue with the intention of selling them immediately at a profit.

Stale bull Someone who has bought shares in anticipation of a quick rise which has not materialised.

Stamp duty A UK tax levied on the purchase of shares with the exception of Government stock and new issues.

Stock A security giving a fixed rate of interest for a fixed period.

Striking price The price at which an option is granted. See Options.

Sweetener A high-yielding stock or share included in a portfolio to raise the average yield overall.

Switch The purchase and sale of investments carried out at the same time to change the composition of the portfolio.

Take-Over One company obtaining control of another by obtaining a majority of the voting shares.

Tap stock Government stock offered for sale by the Government, sometimes to influence the price.

Tender An issue of stocks or shares where prospective buyers specify the price they are willing to pay. The shares are then offered to the highest bidders.

Traded option See Options.

Underwriter Someone, usually a city institution, who agrees to buy any shares in a new issue not purchased by the public.

Unit trust A portfolio of various investments divided into units and managed by professionals. The value of the units does not depend on supply and demand but on the underlying value of the portfolio. For more information contact the Unit Trust Association, Park House, 16 Finsbury Circus, London EC2M 7JP. Tel: 01-638 3071.

Unlisted Securities Market (USM) The stock exchange market for companies who do not qualify or do not wish a full listing. A sort of second-tier market consisting mainly of small companies or recently formed companies. If you pick a winner you could do very well, but it is a high risk investment.

Unsecured loan stock A fixed interest stock not secured by assets.

Warrant A negotiable right to subscribe for stocks or shares at some time in the future. Similar to an option but used by companies to raise money.

Yearlings Bonds issued for twelve months mostly by local authorities.

Yield The gross dividend expressed as a percentage of the share price.

18

18

Stockbrokers

The following is a list by Town of stockbrokers in the UK most of whom are interested in new private clients. They may not all necessarily want to deal with investors who have only £600 or £1,000 to invest though many will – particularly those outside London.

ABERDEEN
Horne & Mackinnon
60 Union Street, Aberdeen AB9 1DH. Tel: 0224-640222.

Parsons & Co
25 Albyn Place, Aberdeen AB1 1YL. Tel: 0224-589345.

William Murray
1 Albyn Terrace, Aberdeen AB9 1RU. Tel: 0224-641307.

ALTRINCHAM
Charterhouse Tilney Ltd
Ashley House, Ashley Road, Altrincham WA14 2DW. Tel: 061-941 4772.

BANGOR
R A Coleman & Co
204 High Street, Bangor, Gwynedd LL57 1NY. Tel: 0248-353242.

BATH
Godfray Derby & Co
1 Northumberland Buildings, Queen Square, Bath, Avon BA1 2JB. Tel: 0225-337100.

BARNSLEY
Stancliffe Ltd
23 Regent Street, Barnsley, S Yorkshire S70 2HH. Tel: 0226-282277/282268.

BARNSTABLE
Milton Mortimer & Co
74 High Street, Barnstable, Devon EX31 1HP. Tel: 0271-71199.

BEDFORD
R N McKean & Co
11 Grove Place, Bedford MK40 3GG. Tel: 0234-51131.

BELFAST
W M F Coates & Co
Northern Bank House, 8/9 Donegall Square, N Belfast BT1 5LX. Tel: 0232-223456.

Josias Cunningham & Co
2 Bridge Street, Belfast BT1 1NX. Tel: 0232-246005.

Laing & Cruickshank
St George's House, 99/101 High Street, Belfast BT1 2AH. Tel: 0232-221002.

BIRMINGHAM
Chambers & Remington
Canterbury House, 85 Newhall Street, Birmingham B3 1LS. Tel: 021-236 2577.

F H F Market Makers Ltd
Charles House, 148/149 Great Charles Street, Birmingham B3 3HT. Tel: 021-236 2211.

Gilbert Jeffs & Co
14 Bennetts Hill, Birmingham B2 5SE. Tel: 021-643 7861/7507.

Griffiths & Lamb
York House, 38 Great Charles Street, Queensway, Birmingham B3 3GY. Tel: 021-236 6641.

Harris Allday Lea & Brooks
33 Great Charles Street, Birmingham B3 3JN. Tel: 021-233 1222.

Murray & Co
Beaufort House, 94 Newhall Street, Birmingham B3 1PE. Tel: 021-236 0891.

Roy Great James & Co
33 Charles Street, Queensway, Birmingham B3 3JS. Tel: 021-236 8131.

Sabin Bacon White & Co
33 Great Charles Street, Queensway, Birmingham B3 3JW. Tel: 021-236 5591.

Smith Keen Cutler
Exchange Buildings, Stephenson Place, Birmingham B2 4NN. Tel: 021-643 9977.

Albert E Sharp & Co
Edmund House, 12 Newhall Street, Birmingham B3 3ER. Tel: 021-236 5801.

Stock Beech & Co
Lloyds Bank Chambers, 75 Edmund Street, Birmingham B3 3HL. Tel: 021-233 3211.

BLACKPOOL
James Brearley & Sons
PO Box 34, 31 King Street, Blackpool FY1 3DQ. Tel: 0253-21474.

Marsden W Hargreave, Hale & Co
PO Box 7, 8 Springfield Road, Blackpool FY1 1QN. Tel: 0253-21575.

BOLTON
Llewellyan, Greenhalgh & Co
20 Mawdsley Street, Bolton BL1 1LF. Tel: 0204-21697.

BOURNEMOUTH
Farley & Thompson
Pine Grange, Bath Road, Bournemouth BH1 2NU. Tel: 0202-26277.

Godfray Derby & Co
Jacey House, The Lansdowne, Bournemouth BH1 2PP. Tel: 0202-25682.

I A Pritchard Ltd
National Westminster Bank Building, 1 Richmond Hill, The Square, Bournemouth BH2 6HW. Tel: 0202-297035.

Robson Cotterell Ltd
Bourne Chambers, St Peters Road, Bournemouth BH1 2JX. Tel: 0202-27581.

BRADFORD
Rensburg & Co
Broadway House, 9 Bank Street, Bradford BD1 1HU. Tel: 0274-729406.

BRISTOL
Heseltine Moss & Co
Stock Exchange Buildings, 34 St Nicholas Street, Bristol BS1 1TW. Tel: 0272-276521.

Hillman Catford Board & Co
45 St Nicholas Street, Bristol BS1 1TX. Tel: 0272-291352/24051.

Laws Queen & Coo
30 Charlotte Street, Bristol BS1 4DU. Tel: 0272-293901.

Stock Beech & Co
The Bristol & West Building, Broad Quay, Bristol BS1 4DD. Tel: 0272-20051.

CAMBRIDGE
Charles Stanley & Co
9 Pembroke Street, Cambridge CB2 3QY. Tel: 0223-316726.

CARDIFF
Heseltine Moss & Co
Pork House, Greyfriars Road, Cardiff CF1 3LB. Tel: 0222-377061.

Lyddon & Co
113 Bute Street, Cardiff CF1 1QS. Tel: 0222-48000.

Murray & Co Stockbrokers Ltd
Westgate House, Westgate Street, Cardiff CF1 1DD. Tel: 0222-397672.

CARLISLE
Stancliffe Ltd
1 Cecil Street, Carlisle CA1 1NL. Tel: 0228-21200.

CHELTENHAM
Henderson Crosthwaite & Co
25 Imperial Square, Cheltenham GL50 1QZ. Tel: 0242-514756.

Heseltine Moss & Co
2 Imperial Square, Cheltenham GL50 1QB. Tel: 0242-571571.

Vivian Gray & Co
Harley House, 29 Cambray Place, Cheltenham GL50 1JN. Tel: 0242 577677.

CHICHESTER
Heseltine Moss & Co
60a North Street, Chichester, W Sussex PO19 1NB. Tel: 0243-786472.

COLCHESTER
A F Matthews & Co
Colne House, 5 George Street, Colchester CO1 1TR. Tel: 0206-549831.

COLWYN BAY
Penney Easton & Co
15 Wynnstay Road, Colwyn Bay, N Wales LL29 8NN. Tel: 0492-30354.

COVENTRY
Credit Suisse Buckmaster & Moore
66 Queens Road, Coventry CV1 3FU. Tel: 0203-25352.

DERBY
Stevenson & Barrs
P O Box 63, 10/12 James St, Derby. Tel: 0332-47451/32425.

DORCHESTER
Richardson Chubb & Co
5 High West Street, Dorchester, Dorset DT1 1UJ. Tel: 0305-65252.

DUNDEE
Parsons & Co
51 Meadowside, Dundee DD1 9PQ. Tel: 0382-21081

EASTBOURNE
Laing & Cruickshank
12 Gildredge Road, Eastbourne, East Sussex BN21 4RL. Tel: 0323-20893/31656.

EDINBURGH
Bell Lawrie & Co
PO Box 8, Erskine House, 68 Queen Street, Edinburgh EH2 4AE. Tel: 031-225 2566.

Parsons & Co
12 Melville Crescent, Edinburgh EH3 7LU. Tel: 031-226 4466.

Penney Easton & Co
21 Dublin Street, Edinburgh EH1 3RF. Tel: 031-556 1195.

Torrie & Co
6 Hope Street, Edinburgh EH2 4DB. Tel: 031-225 1766.

Wood Mackenzie Private Client Services Ltd
Kintore House, 74/77 Queen Street, Edinburgh EH2 4NS. Tel: 031-225 8525.

EXETER
Henry J Garratt & Co
Broadwalk House, Southernhay, Exeter EX1 1TS. Tel: 0392-52679.

Milton Mortimer & Co
21 Southernay West, Exeter EX1 1PR. Tel: 0392-76244/58255.

GLASGOW
Campbell Neill & Co
Stock Exchange House, 69 St Georges Place, Glasgow G2 1JN. Tel: 041-248 6271.

Carswell & Co
69 St Georges Place, Glasgow G2 1BU. Tel: 041-221 3402.

Laing & Cruickshank
De Quincey House, 48 West Regent Street, Glasgow G2 2RB. Tel: 041-333 9323.

Parsons & Co
100 West Nile Street, Glagow G1 2QU. Tel: 041-332 8791.

Penney Easton & Co
24 George Square, Glasgow G2 1EB. Tel: 041-248 2911.

Speirs & Jeffrey
36 Renfield Street, Glasgow G2 1NA. Tel: 041-248 4311.

Stirling Hendry & Co
16 Royal Exchange Square, Glasgow G1 3AD. Tel: 041-248 6033.

GLOUCESTER
Heseltine Moss & Co
2 Beaufort Buildings, Spa Road, Gloucester GL1 1XB. Tel: 0452-25444.

GUERNSEY
Credit Suisse Buckmaster & Moore (Guernsey) Ltd
28A Commercial Arcade, St Peter Port, Guernsey. Tel: 0481-710441.

Sheppards and Chase
Suite 374E, Hirzel Court, St Peter Port, Guernsey. Tel: 0481-28950.

HALIFAX
Broadbridge Lawson & Co
Fountain Chambers, Fountain Street, Halifax HX1 1LS. Tel: 0422-67707.

HARROGATE
Cawood Smithie & Co
22 East Parade, Harrogate, N Yorkshire HG1 5LT. Tel: 0423-66781/522226.

Stancliffe Ltd
Claremont House, Victoria Avenue, Harrogate, N Yorkshire HG1 5QQ. Tel: 0423-66071.

HARTLEPOOL
Cawood Smithie & Co
73 Church Street, Hartlepool, Cleveland TS24 7DN. Tel: 0429-272231/274491.

HEREFORD
Henderson Crosthwaite & Co
27 King Street, Hereford HR4 9BX. Tel: 0432-265647.

Vivian Gray & Co
35 Bridge Street, Hereford HR4 9DG. Tel: 0432-53491.

HORSHAM
Henderson Crosthwaite & Co
Central House, Medwin Walk, Horsham RH12 1AG. Tel: 0403-61167.

HUDDERSFIELD
Battye, Wimpenny & Dawson
Woodsome House, Woodsome Park, Fenacy Bridge, Huddersfield HD8 0JG. Tel: 0484-608066.

Robert Ramsden & Co
PO Box B16, Estate Buildings (1st Floor), Railway Street, Huddersfield HD1 1NE. Tel: 0484-21501.

HULL
Stancliffe Ltd
Middleton Chambers, Lowgate, Hull, N Humberside HU1 1EA. Tel: 0482-226293/23935.

Fowler Sutton & Co
PO Box 10, 35 Bishop Lane, Hull HU1 1NZ. Tel: 0482-25750.

IPSWICH
Charles Stanley & Co
16 Northgate Street, Ipswich, Suffolk IP1 3DB. Tel: 0473-210264.

Vivian Gray & Co
23 Lower Brook Street, Ipswich, Suffolk IP4 1AQ. Tel: 0473-225075.

ISLE OF MAN
Credit Suisse Buckmaster & Moore (IOM) Ltd
3 Athol Street, Douglas, Isle of Man. Tel: 0624-27134.

Ramsey Crookall & Co
25 Atholl Street, Douglas, Isle of Man. Tel: 0624-73171.

R L Stott & Co
Exchange House, 54–58 Athol Street, Douglas, Isle of Man. Tel: 0624-73701.

JERSEY
Brewin Dolphin & Co
Caversham House, 19 Queen Street, St Helier, Jersey. Tel: 0534-27391/2/3

James Capel (Channel Islands) Ltd
5 Britannia Place, St Helier, Jersey. Tel: 0534-77077.

Charlton Seal Dimmock & Co
Channel House, Green Street, St Helier, Jersey, CI. Tel: 0534-25225.

Charterhouse-Tilney
PO Box 348, Charterhouse Building, Bath Street, St Helier, Jersey. Tel: 0534-79437.

Hoare Govett (Jersey) Ltd
PO Box 1, 35 Don Street, St Helier, Jersey. Tel: 0534-77548.

Le Masurier James & Chinn
PO Box 16, 29 Broad Street, St
Helier, Jersey. Tel: 0534-72825.

Sheppards and Chase
12 Esplanade, St Helier, Jersey.
Tel: 0534-76222.

Stancliffe Ltd
Industria House, Red Houses, St
Brelade, Jersey. Tel: 0534-
45567.

LANCASTER
Hanson & Co
66 Church Street, Lancaster LA1
1LW. Tel: 0245-32582.

LEEDS
Broadbridge Lawson & Co
16 Park Place, Leeds LS1 2SJ.
Tel: 0532-443721.

Howitt & Pemberton
17th Floor, Royal Exchange
House, Boar Lane, Box No 85,
Leeds LS1 5NS. Tel: 0532-
439011/450531.

Redmayne-Bentley
Merton House, 84 Albion Street,
Leeds LS1 6AG. Tel: 0532-
436941.

Rensburg & Co
11 Park Square East, Leeds LS1
2NG. Tel: 0532-434631.

Wise Speke & Co
Provincial House, 28 Albion
Street, Leeds LS1 5AL. Tel: 0532-
459341.

LEICESTER
Hill Osborne & Co
Permanent House, Horsefair
Street, Leicester LE1 5BU. Tel:
0533-29185.

Wiltshire Baldwin & Co
19 The Crescent, King Street,
Leicester LE1 6RX. Tel: 0533-
541344.

LINCOLN
Hill Osborne & Co
Royal Insurance Building, Silver
Street, Lincoln LN2 1DU. Tel:
0522-28244.

LIVERPOOL
Ashton Tod McLaren
13 Castle Street, Liverpool L2
4SU. Tel: 051-236 8281.

Blankstone Sington & Co
Martins Buildings, 6 Water
Street, Liverpool L2 3SP. Tel:
051-227 1881.

Charterhouse-Tilney
385 Sefton House, Exchange
Buildings, Liverpool L2 3RT. Tel:
052-236 6000.

Neilson Milnes
Martins Building, 4 Water Street,
Liverpool L2 3UF. Tel: 051-236
9891.

Rensburg & Co
Silkhouse, Tithebarn Street,
Liverpool L2 2NH. Tel: 051-227
2030.

LONDON
Anderson & Co
62 London Wall, London EC2R
7DQ. Tel: 01-638 1200.

Astaire & Co Ltd
117 Bishopsgate, London EC2M
3TD. Tel: 01-283 2081.

Barclays de Zoete Wedd
PO Box 188, Ebbgate House, 2
Swan Lane, London EC4R 3TS.
Tel: 01-623 4321.

A J Bekhor & Co
12a Finsbury Square, London
EC2A 1LT. Tel: 01-628 6050.

Brewin Dolphin & Co
5 Giltspur Street, London EC1A
9DE. Tel. 01-248 4400.

Campbell Neill & Co
City Gate House, 39 Finsbury
Square, London EC2A 1PX. Tel:
01-920 9661.

James Capel & Co
PO Box 551, 6 Bevis Marks, London EC3A 7JQ. Tel: 01-621 0011.

Capel Cure Myers
65 Holborn Viaduct, London
EC1A 2EU. Also at the Stock
Exchange, London EC2N 1HP.
Tel: 01-236 5080.

Charterhouse-Tilney Ltd
1 Warnford Court, Throgmorton
Street, London EC2N 2AT. Tel:
01-638 0683.

Chase Manhattan Securities
PO Box 152, Portland House,
72/73 Basinghall Street, London
EC2V 5DP. Tel: 01-606 6622.

Cobbold & Roach & Co
66 Cornhill, London EC3V 3NB.
Tel: 01-626 1601.

Coni Gilbert & Sankey
10 Throgmorton Avenue, Throgmorton Street, London EC2N
2DH. Tel: 01-638 8871.

T C Coombs & Co
22 City Road, London EC1Y 2AG.
Tel: 01-628 5070.

County Securities Ltd
Drapers Gardens, 12 Throgmorton Avenue, London EC2P 2ES.
Tel: 01-382-1000.

Credit Suisse Buckmaster & Moore
80 Cannon Street, London EC4N
6HH. Tel: 01-588 2868.

Dennis Murphy Campbell & Co
2 Russell Row, London EC2V
8BP. Tel: 01-726 8631.

John M Douglas & Eykyn Brothers
30 College Street, London EC4R
2TE. Tel: 01-248 4277.

Dunkley Marshall
4 London Wall Buildings, London EC2M 5NX. Tel: 01-638
1282.

Earnshaw, Haes & Sons
17 Tokenhouse Yard, London
EC2R 7LB. Tel: 01-588 5699.

J M Finn & Co
Salisbury House, London Wall,
EC2M 5TA. Tel: 01-628 9688.

Foster & Braithwaite
22 Austin Friars, London EC2N
2BU. Tel: 01-588 6111.

Henry J Garratt & Co
34 Copthall Avenue, London
EC2R 7BB. Tel: 01-628 9232/
9545.

Granville Davies Coleman Ltd
27/28 Lovat Lane, London EC3R
8EB. Tel: 01-621 1212.

Godfray Derby & Co
6 Broad Street Place, London
EC2M 7LH. Tel: 01-638 0767.

Goodbody Dudgeon
Warnford Court, Throgmorton
Street, London EC2N 2AT. Tel:
01-628 4131.

Vivian Gray & Co
10 Dominion Street, London
EC2M 2UX. Tel: 01-638 2888.

Greene & Co
Bilbao House, 36 New Broad
Street, London EC4M 9EL. Tel:
01-628 7241.

W Greenwell Montagu & Co
Bow Bells House, Bread Street,
London EC4M 9EL. Tel: 01-236-
2040.

Greig Middleton & Co
78 Old Broad Street, London
EC2M 1JE. Tel: 01-920 0481.

Guidehouse Securities Ltd
Vestry House, Greyfriars Pas-
sage, Newgate St, London EC1A
7BA. Tel: 01-606 6321.

Henderson Crosthwaite & Co
194 Bishopsgate, London EC2M
4LL. Tel: 01-283 8577.

Heseltine Moss & Co
3 Trump Street, London EC2V
8DH. Tel: 01-606 1401.

Hill Osborne & Co
Warnford Court, Throgmorton
Street, London EC2N 2AT. Tel:
01-628 2205.

Hitchens Harrison & Co
Bell Court House, 11 Blomfield
Street, London EC2M 1LB. Tel:
01-588 5171/1936.

**Hoare Govett Financial Services
Ltd**
319/325 High Holborn, London
WC1V 7PB. Tel: 01-404 0344.

Illingworth & Henriques Ltd
Wardgate House, 59a London
Wall, London EC2M 5UA. Tel:
01-638 0801.

Jacobson Townsely & Co
4th Floor, Friars House, 39 New
Broad Street, London EC2M
1NH. Tel: 01-638 6671.

G H & A M Jay
61 Cheapside, London EC2. Tel:
01-248 0081.

Keith Bayley Rogers & Co
194 Bishopsgate, London EC2M
4NR. Tel: 01-623 2400.

Kitcat & Aitken
17th Floor, Stock Exchange, London EC2N 1HB. Tel: 01-588 6280.

Kleinwort Grieveson & Co
PO Box 191, 10 Fenchurch
Street, London EC3M 3LB. Tel:
01-623 8000.

Laing & Cruickshank
Piercy House, 7 Copthall Avenue, London EC2R 7BE. Tel:
01-588 2800.

Laurence Keen & Co
Basildon House, 7–11 Moorgate,
London EC2R 6AH. Tel: 01-600
9100.

Laurence Prust & Co
Basildon House, 7–11 Moorgate,
London EC2R 6AH and The
Stock Exchange, London EC2N
1HB. Tel: 01-606 6811.

Le Mare Martin & Co
City Gate House, 4th Floor, 39
Finsbury Square, London EC2A
1LE. Tel: 01-628 9472.

Margetts & Addenbrooke
65 London Wall, London EC2M
5TU. Tel: 01-588 0421.

Merrill Lynch Ltd
Merrill Lynch House, 27 Finsbury Square, London EC2A 1AQ. Tel: 01-382 8000.

L Messel & Co
1 Finsbury Avenue, London EC2M 2QE. Tel: 01-377 0123.

Montague Loebl Stanley Financial Services
31 Sun Street, London EC2M 2QP. Tel: 01-377 9242.

Murray & Co Stockbrokers
City Gate House, 39/45 Finsbury Square, London EC2A 1PX. Tel: 01-588 5386/2688.

Northgate & Co
119 Finsbury Pavement, London EC2A 1JJ. Tel: 01-628 8121.

Orme & Co
Warnford Court, Throgmorton Street, London EC2N 2BD. Tel: 01-638 0991.

Penney Easton & Co
3 St Helens Place, London EC3A 6AU. Tel: 01-628 9321.

Phillips & Drew Investment Services Ltd
Mercury House, Triton Court, 14 Finsbury Square, London EC2A 1PD. Tel: 01-628 4444.

Quilter Goodison Co Ltd
31 Gresham Street, London EC2V 7LH. Tel: 01-600 4177.

Savory Mill
3 London Wall Buildings, London EC2M 5PU. Tel: 01-638 1212.

Schaverien & Co
18½ Sekforde Street, London EC1R 0HN. Tel: 01-251 1626.

Paul E Schweder, Miller & Co
46/50 Sun Street, London EC2M 2PX. Tel: 01-588 5600.

Albert E Sharp
6/7 Queen Street, London EC4N 1SP. Tel: 01-248 8678.

Shaw & Co
4 London Wall Buildings, Blomfield Street, London EC2M 5NT. Tel: 01-638 3644.

Sheppards & Chase
Clements House, Gresham Street, London EC2V 7AU. Tel: 01-606 8099.

Smith New Court Agency Ltd
Salisbury House, London Wall, London EC2M 5SX. Tel: 01-628 4433.

Southard Gilbey McNish & Co
65 London Wall, London EC2M 5TU. Tel: 01-638 6761.

Spencer Thornton & Co
29 Throgmorton Street, London EC2N 2JU. Tel: 01-628 4411.

Springer Bale & Lewis
110 Warnford Court, Throgmorton Street, London EC2N 2BB. Tel: 01-628 9941/8322.

Stancliffe Ltd
29 Throgmorton Street, London EC2N 2AT. Tel: 01-628 3321.

Charles Stanley & Co
18 Finsbury Circus, London EC2M 7BL. Tel: 01-638 5717.

Sternberg Thomas Clarke & Co
218 Bishopsgate, London EC2M 4QD. Tel: 01-247 8461.

Strauss Turnbull & Co Ltd
3 Moorgate Place, London EC2R
6HR. Tel: 01-638 5699.

Teather & Greenwood
Austin Friars House, 2–6 Austen
Friars, London EC2N 2EE.
Tel: 01-628 0321.

R J Thompson
1 Salisbury Buildings, London
Wall, London EC2M 5RH. Tel:
01-588 2790.

Helbert Wagg & Co
(Anderson Bryce Villiers Ltd)
9 Devonshire Square, London
EC2M 4YL. Tel: 01-623 4500.

Walker Crips Weddle Beck & Co
152 City Road, London EC1V
2PQ. Tel: 01-253 7502.

Westons Securities Ltd
8/9 Botolph Alley, London EC3R
8DR. Tel: 01-283 8466.

**Williams de Broë Hill Chaplin &
Co**
Pinners Hall, Austin Friars, London EC2P 2HS. Tel: 01-588 7511.

Russell Wood & Co
Kennet House, Kennet Wharf
Lane, Upper Thames Street,
London EC4V 3AJ. Tel: 01-236
3761.

Raphael, Zorn
10 Throgmorton Avenue, London EC2N 2DP. Tel: 01-628 4000.

LONDONDERRY
D M Wright & Partners
15 The Diamond, Londonderry
BT48 6HW Northern Ireland. Tel:
0504-263344.

MANCHESTER
Ashworth Sons & Barratt
26 Pall Mall, Manchester M2
1LS. Tel: 061-832 4812.

Bell Houldsworth & Co
4 Norfolk Street, Manchester
M60 2QL. Tel: 061-834 3542.

Charlton Seal Dimmock & Co
76 Cross Street, Manchester
M60 2EP. Tel: 061-832 3488.

Henry Cooke Lumsden Ltd
PO Box 369, 1 King Street, Manchester M60 3AH. Tel: 061-834
2332.

Gall & Eke
10 Charlotte Street, Manchester
M1 4FL. Tel: 061-228 2511.

Gartside & Trippier Ltd
2 Old Bank Chambers, St Ann's
Square, Manchester M2 7PF.
Tel: 061-834 6084.

Illingworth & Henriques Ltd
PO Box 419, 38/40 Kennedy
Street, Manchester M60 2BP.
Tel: 061-236 8521.

W H Ireland & Co
Dennis House, Marsden Street,
Manchester M2 1HL. Tel: 061-
832 2174/834 6325.

Piling Trippier & Co
12 St Anns Square, Manchester
M2 7HT. Tel: 061-832 6581.

John Siddall & Son
4 Norfolk Street, Manchester M2
1DS. Tel: 061-832 7471.

Arnold Stansby & Co
Dennis House, Marsden Street,
Manchester M2 3JJ. Tel: 061-
832 8554.

MIDDLESBROUGH
Cawood Smithie & Co
48a High Street, Stokesley, Middlesbrough, Cleveland TS9 5AX. Tel: 0642-712771.

Stancliffe Ltd
206 Marton Road, Middlesbrough, Cleveland TS4 2JE. Tel: 0642-249211.

Wise Speke & Co
103 Albert Road, Middlesbrough, Cleveland TS1 2PA. Tel: 0642-248431.

NEWBURY
Heseltine Moss & Co
25 Bartholomew Street, Newbury RG14 5LL. Tel: 0635-37800.

NEWRY
Magennis & Co
43 Lower Mill Street, Newry BT34 1AH. Tel: 0693-4314.

NEWCASTLE-UPON-TYNE
Penney Easton & Co
1 Collingwood Buildings, Collingwood Street, Newcastle-upon-Tyne NE1 1JF. Tel: 091-261 9957.

Wise Speke & Co
Commercial Union House, 39 Pilgrim Street, Newcastle-upon-Tyne NE1 6RQ. Tel: 091-261 1266.

NORTHAMPTON
Cave & Sons
9–11 Hazelwood Road, Northampton NN1 1LQ. Tel: 0604-21421.

NORWICH
Barratt & Cooke
5 Opie Street, Norwich NR1 3DW. Tel: 0603-624236.

Waters Luniss & Co
5 Queen Street, Norwich NR2 4SG. Tel: 0603-622265.

NOTTINGHAM
William Chapman Trease & Co
Norwich Union House, South Parade, Nottingham NG1 2LN. Tel: 0602-476772.

OXFORD
Heseltine Moss & Co
4 King Edward Street, Oxford OX1 4HJ. Tel: 0865-243581.

PERTH
Penney Easton & Co
4 Charlotte Street, Perth PH1 5LL. Tel: 0738-37441/73817.

PETERBOROUGH
Credit Suisse Buckmaster & Moore
88 Lincoln Road, Peterborough PE1 2SN. Tel: 0733-311611.

PLYMOUTH
Westlake & Co (Stockbrokers) Ltd
Princess House, Eastlake Walk, Plymouth PL1 1HG. Tel: 0752-220971.

POOLE
A J Bekhor & Co
153 High Street, Poole, Dorset BH15 1AU. Tel: 0202-678081.

Godfray Derby & Co
38 Parkstone Road, Poole, Dorset BH15 2PG. Tel: 0202-676433.

READING
Helseltine Moss & Co
30 Friar Street, Reading, Berks RG1 1AH. Tel: 0734-595511.

SALISBURY
Vivian Gray & Co
45–55 Milford Street, Salisbury, Wiltshire SP1 2BP. Tel: 0722-330333.

SCARBOROUGH
Hill Osborne & Co
17 York Place, Scarborough YO11 2NP. Tel: 0723-372478.

SHEFFIELD
Nicholson Barber & Co
PO Box 132, Fargate Court, Fargate, Sheffield S1 1LE. Tel: 0742-755100.

Walter Ward & Co
11 Norfolk Row, Sheffield .S1 2PA. Tel: 0742-22292.

SOUTHAMPTON
Cobbold Roach & Co
61 Devonshire Road, Southampton SO9 1XL. Tel: 0703-333292.

SOUTHPORT
Charlton Brett & Boughey
P O Box 23, 367 Lord St, Southport, Merseyside PR8 1NS. Tel: 0704-32282.

STIRLING
Penny Easton & Co
18 Maxwell Close, Stirling, Scotland SK8 1JU. Tel: 0786 73817.

STOCKPORT
McLellan Ballard & Co
2–6 Norbury Street, Stockport SK1 3SH. Tel: 061-480 3906/3035.

STOKE-ON-TRENT
P H Pope & Son
6 Pall Mall, Hanley, Stoke-on-Trent. Tel: 0782-251154.

SUNDERLAND
Stancliffe Ltd
57 John Street, Sunderland, Tyne & Wear SR1 1QH. Tel: 0783-657575.

SWANSEA
Heseltine Moss & Co
6 Caer Street, Swansea SA1 1DD. Tel: 0792-54907.

TAUNTON
Laing & Cruickshank
4 Mendip House, High Street, Taunton, Somerset TA1 3SX. Tel: 0823-54351.

TIVERTON
Vivian Gray & Co
The Clock House, East Anstley, Nr Tiverton, Devon EX16 9JB. Tel: 0398-4393.

TORQUAY
Whale Hardaway & Co
5 Parkhill Road, Torquay TQ1 2AN. Tel: 0803-22441.

TRURO
Vivian Gray & Co
Eagle Star House, Lemon Street, Truro, Cornwall TR1 2PX. Tel: 0872-75454.

TUNBRIDGE WELLS
T C Coombs & Co
5 York Road, Tunbridge Wells, Kent TN1 1JX. Tel: 0892-39501.

WAKEFIELD
Broadbridge Lawson & Co
19 King Street, Wakefield WF1 2SP. Tel: 0924-372601/371504.

WELLS
Godfray Derby & Co
Penniless Porch, Market Place, Wells, Somerset BA5 1DJ. Tel: 0749-76373.

WESTCLIFF-ON-SEA
Henry J Garratt & Co
67 Hamlet Court Road, Westcliff-on-Sea, Essex SS0 7EU. Tel: 0702-347173.

WINCHESTER
Cobbold Roach & Co
3 St Peters Street, Winchester, Hants SO23 8BJ. Tel: 0962-52362.

WORCESTER
Henderson Crosthwaite & Co
Virginia House, The Butts, Worcester. Tel: 0905-29551.

YORK
Greig Middleton & Co
23 Petergate, York YO1 2HS. Tel: 0904-647911.

Final Thoughts

Success is just a matter of luck – ask any failure.
Earl Wilson

Making money can be fun, and after a certain point it can
bring more money.
Neil Simon

Anyone who thinks there's safety in numbers hasn't
looked at the Stock Market pages.
Irene Peter

There are few ways in which a man can be more
innocently employed than in getting money.
Samuel Johnson

He has so much money that he could afford to look poor.
Edgar Wallace

Index

THE
SAVERS AND
INVESTORS GUIDE

David Lewis's comprehensive guide contains invaluable information to help cut your tax bill, perhaps by hundreds of pounds, as well as lots of sound detailed advice on where best to save and invest your money.

Previously sold under the title **Money Mail Savers' Guide**, **it has sold over 300,000 copies**. In clear no-nonsense language, this fact-packed book analyses 78 different types of savings and investments. **Not to be missed**.

Recommended by the Sunday Times, Daily Express, Financial Times, The Observer, The Times, The Guardian, Choice Magazine, Citizens' Advice Bureaux, Ideal Home magazine, Yorkshire Post.

ASK YOUR BOOKSHOP FOR COPIES OR USE THE ORDER FORM BELOW

To: **Wisebuy Publications, 25 West Cottages, London NW6 1RJ**

Please send me _____ copies of THE SAVERS AND INVESTORS GUIDE at £2.95 a copy plus 50p p&p or £6 airmail including p&p.

Please send me _____ copies of SHARES – A BEGINNERS' GUIDE TO MAKING MONEY at £2.95 per copy plus 50p p&p or £6 airmail including p&p.

Please send me _____ copies of BUYING SELLING AND MOVING HOME at £3.50 a copy plus 50p p&p or £6 airmail including p&p.

I enclose cheque/PO for £ _____ payable to Wisebuy Publications

Name_____
Block letters please

Address_____

_____

_____ Post code _____ SH2

BUYING, SELLING AND MOVING HOME

DAVID LEWIS

'One of the best books ever written
for would-be homebuyers.'
Daily Telegraph

'Young people planning to buy their first
own home will find some worthwhile reading.'
Sunday Times

**'This is the sort of book that could save you many times over
what you spend on it, not to mention the savings it will
help you make in emotional worry.'**
Huddersfield Daily Examiner

'. . . covers most aspects of the home owning
process in a clear manner which will be
helpful to the layperson.'
Law Society's Gazette

'A useful new book.'
The Guardian

'Throughout the book there are useful hints
on how to save money and how
to calculate possibly unforseen costs.'
National Council of Citizens' Advice Bureaux

'. . . invaluable in explaining and advising on house purchase
or selling, gazumping, conveyancing and how to
look for the best bargain.'
Glasgow Herald

**Published in the Teach Yourself Series, copies of Buying
Selling and Moving Home by David Lewis are also available by
post from Wisebuy Publications using the order form overleaf.**